SHUT UP AND SELL YOUR FIRST BOOK

SECRETS TO LEVERAGE

48 WAYS TO MARKET YOUR WAY TO SUCCESS

NATASA DENMAN

First published by Ultimate World Publishing 2021
Copyright © 2021 Natasa Denman

ISBN
Paperback - 978-1-922597-11-3
Ebook - 978-1-922597-14-4

Natasa Denman has asserted her rights under the Copyright, Designs and Patents Act 1988 to be identified as the author of this work. The information in this book is based on the author's experiences and opinions. The publisher specifically disclaims responsibility for any adverse consequences which may result from use of the information contained herein. Permission to use information has been sought by the author. Any breaches will be rectified in further editions of the book.

All rights reserved. No part of this publication may be reproduced, stored in or introduced into a retrieval system, or transmitted in any form, or by any means (electronic, mechanical, photocopying, recording or otherwise) without the prior written permission of the author. Any person who does any unauthorised act in relation to this publication may be liable to criminal prosecution and civil claims for damages. Enquiries should be made through the publisher.

Cover design: Ultimate World Publishing
Layout and typesetting: Ultimate World Publishing
Editor: Marinda Wilkinson

Ultimate World Publishing
Diamond Creek,
Victoria Australia 3089
www.writeabook.com.au

'I met Natasa Denman in August 2018 and attended the Ultimate 48 Hour Author Retreat the following year in May 2019. I was nervous, frightened but enormously excited to be embarking on a journey to realise a dream I'd had since I was in high school. The support and guidance Natasa gave me, not only helped me achieve my dream of writing *The Unexpected Journey*, but also allowed me to see how much more I have to offer to people embarking on the same journey as me.

She doesn't teach anything she hasn't tried herself. Her energy is infectious and her lessons invaluable. I am now writing my second book and look forward to an amazing future because of Natasa and her belief in me.'

Julie Fisher, Author of the *Unexpected Journey*

'Nat is a stupendous resource from the beginning to the finish line. She has taught me proven and evidence-based strategies on how to leverage your book and capitalise on your ideas. She will guide you in monetising your ideas through other streams of income.'

Nicole Guevara, Author of *Breakaway*

'I followed Nat's advice to drop some teaser Facebook posts in the days leading up to the Ultimate 48 Hour Retreat and then pre-released on the first night of retreat. I had over 70 sales before my book was published! That's a great conversion considering I only had 160 Facebook friends at the time.'

**Jennifer Emmett,
Author of *Beyond Possible***

'One of the smartest things I learned in my 30 years of running a successful business from home was to hire smarter people to do the jobs that I wasn't an expert in – and I found the authoring experts in Natasa and the Ultimate 48 Hour Author team! Boy was I lucky to see that little ad on Facebook because 13 weeks later our book was in hand.

Not only did we get a 10-year-old idea completed but I was renewed with a magical energy and creativity that I had long lost for my business. The whole business looks new again and I am happier than I've been in a long time.'

Renae Kunda, Co-Author of *King of the Cape*

'Natasa highlights the importance of both online and offline marketing and sales of a book and practical examples of each during her training which has been an important part of my overall strategy. I've learned how to look out for opportunities to promote and share my book with a wide variety of people around the world and this has been very useful in a global pandemic.'

Krissy Regan, Author of *Broken to Unbreakable*

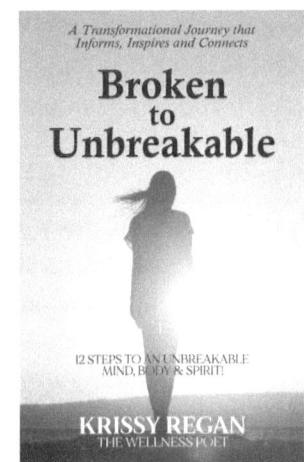

'Writing my first book has been only part of the journey – and it has been so much more exciting and successful because of the support and strategies from Natasa and Ultimate 48 Hour Author.

As soon as my book was printed, I was excited to post out 36 copies which had been pre-sold. Marketing the book before writing it had a two-fold benefit – I had made those sales which made me accountable to finish the book, and I also had some funds coming in straight away.

My book was published just four months after the retreat and I sold many more copies at my book launch a couple of months later. Even people who had already purchased it came along and bought more copies as gifts for friends, family or clients.

Once the ball started rolling, I made sure that I followed the recipe Natasa teaches regarding marketing. I attended all the Masterclasses and even got the help of Ultimate 48 Hour Author to become a #1 Amazon Best Seller!

Mother's Day in May 2020 was a wonderful time to package up a book special with a styling service voucher. I enjoyed packaging these up beautifully and sold another 20 copies of the book.

Since publishing I have had many speaking engagements. Even during COVID-19, I have been able to present to groups on Zoom calls. Marketing and sales has never been something I was interested in, however, the mentoring from Ultimate 48 Hour Author has provided me with many ideas and strategies. The main benefit from writing a book has been the ongoing support: the Masterclasses and Monday sessions as well as the many other videos and files provided help so much with marketing and sales. The experience has been invaluable for more than just writing the book. It carries through into so much more.'

Moana Robinson, Author of *B Styled for Life*

'In 2015 I was in a low place. I had previously been on top of the world, created many successful businesses, but now faced extreme medical conditions and nearly died. I had almost lost everything, let people down and I felt suicidal. However, Natasa and Stuart showed me a pathway out of that depression: to share the experiences I have had over 40 years in business. So, I wrote a book. Guided by Nat and her system and a lot of encouragement, I wrote a book that has not only brought me back from the brink, but has also helped many businesses and organisations all over the world. Thanks Nat!'

Tony Park, International Best Selling Author, Entrepreneur & Academic

'Natasa teaches authors that running "magnetic events" sells the most books.

In her Masterclasses her KEY to targeting an audience with what's on offer, is the use of sexy words to draw them in, *e.g. "How to lose 10 kilos in 3 days by eating chocolate"*!!! This can be a metaphor, but figures give more power! As Nat says, "You need to create an empowering message so they will be clambering to buy your book".

Be dynamic! Tell them what they want to hear. Wishy washy words won't cut it, so share your best tips. Your audience want to come away being enthused. Nat's strategy is that events need to be CURIOSITY DRIVEN. To get Bums on Seats, people want to come along (and ultimately buy books) with the knowledge that they will be gaining something for themselves, *e.g. "When you come to my event and buy my book, you are going to learn 1, 2, 3, 4!"* In establishing the takeaway, you establish value before talking price!

This was a GOLDEN NUGGET of information for me. I was excited to have written a book, but learning how to get it out there in the most efficient and enjoyable way was paramount, and Nat delivered this in a dynamic way.'

Glenda Wise, Author of *The World is Your Pearl*

DEDICATION

To the coronavirus pandemic and Melbourne lockdowns. If it wasn't for you, I wouldn't have been brave enough to pivot my business fully online and become location independent.

You gave me three lockdowns with collectively six months without leaving my house. This enabled me to set up the new online success systems, practise my craft via Zoom, spread my business successfully within the USA and Canada, pay off my house, buy another house, hire an extra person into the business and write this book.

While others thought you would go away quickly, I fought for the survival of my family and business. You made me think 'outside the box', gave me time with loved ones and a rest from a decade of non-stop national and international travel.

Now, I am ready to be with people again so can you please go away …

CONTENTS

Dedication ix
Introduction xiii

PART 1: 48 Strategies to Market Your Way to Success 1

    SECTION 1: Pre-Launch Success 3

    SECTION 2: Book in Hand 17

    SECTION 3: Hi-Touch Success (Offline Exposure & Power) 29

    SECTION 4: Hi-Tech Success (Online Exposure & Power) 77

    SECTION 5: Scale Up (Time for Leverage) 103

PART 2: Strategies from Real-Life Authors
Getting Real-Life Results 141

    SECTION 6: Real-Life Authors Getting Real-Life Results 143

    Afterword 163

    About the Author 165

    Explore 169

INTRODUCTION

Someone said, 'It takes a bloody long time not to write a book!' and I agree. But it you have picked up this book, it means you have written your book (or are about to write it) and are looking for a way to move your books out of your garage. Most likely you chose the route of self-publishing and invested your hard-earned cash to bring it to reality. Congratulations! Most people never muster up the courage to take the journey of fulfilling that lifelong dream of becoming a first-time published author.

According to writer Joseph Epstein, '81 per cent of Americans feel that they have a book in them – and should write it'. That's approximately 200 million people who aspire to authorship just in the US alone. Less than 0.01% will ever do it and from that only 0.025% will sell more than 1000 books. The reality is a book alone won't put food on the table. For you to succeed financially with your book, you will need to do a lot more than just write it.

The first thing I want to say is that your book is not the magic bullet.

You are! **https://tinyurl.com/magicbulletyou**

The secret to book sales and marketing success lives within you. I believe that every single book can bring success to the author when they take the right actions, put in the effort and remain consistent over a long period of time. The reason so many books fail to become a success is not that they're poorly written, it is that the author never bothered to let people know that they have actually written a book. We all know that you can be the best at something or create an amazing product, but if nobody knows about it, it will never become a success – it will stay the best kept secret.

As a self-published author, I have written 13 books over the past decade. I have also helped over 500 first-time authors complete and publish their first books via our Ultimate 48 Hour Author signature system. I have mentored, supported and observed their journeys beyond the publishing of their books for many years. What you're about to read in this book is the unpacking of those observations, the traits I have found successful authors have and the strategies that have been implemented which enabled them to arrive at that success.

In this book I will share with you the 48 most powerful ways to market and sell your book. The key to your success lies within how many of the strategies you action and implement. Implementing 5 to 10 of them will not get you to success. Implementing and actioning more than half of the 48 strategies will get you closer. And if you take your time and give everything I suggest a go, your success will be guaranteed.

In today's world relying solely upon book sales is a difficult and draining journey to undertake. As authors we need to think bigger! We have a story, message or a form of expertise that we aim to share on a global scale, to make an impact on other people's lives. Authors are change makers. They are people that want to help other people and make the world a nicer place to live in.

INTRODUCTION

The types of books that this book will be most relevant to are the expertise/how-to style books and the legacy/life story books. If you have written a fiction or children's book, you will still benefit from some of the suggestions and ideas in this book, but I recommend you also learn and read further from the authors who have succeeded in those genres.

I often talk about your book being your business. Those that are writing their life story find it challenging to connect with the business, marketing and selling aspects of what I teach. If this is you, I highly recommend that you challenge yourself to think bigger and outside of your story. Check out this live stream I did recently: **https://tinyurl.com/valueinyourstory**

Every single story has value, words of wisdom and a signature system behind it of what that particular person has done to overcome their challenges. This is where the value lies. People relate to stories, but within those stories they are looking for the answer to the question: What's in it for me? This is where your signature system and the way you have overcome your trauma, hardship or obstacles in solving a particular problem becomes of great value to someone else's life.

As we begin this journey together, I want to unpack the top 10 traits successful authors have. Without resolving your mindset blocks behind selling and marketing yourself, you will always stand in your own way to success. This is coming from my personal experience and the successful authors I have helped build 6–7 figure businesses behind their books.

1. Listen, follow the recipe and take action
2. Understand that success is a slow burn process
3. Take action consistently not sporadically
4. Understand that your network is your net worth
5. Build further offers behind their book

6. Write more books
7. Plaster their author status everywhere
8. Get over themselves and share their story and expertise
9. Help others succeed
10. Ask for help, invest in help and continue learning further on sales and marketing

These are going to be your goal posts in terms of mindset and how you need to show up each and every single day. The journey ahead won't be easy, but I can guarantee it will be worth it. Things will get easier with repetition and mastery of skills you once found to be alien to you. As my mum always taught me: 'Every beginning is hard.' The first two years will be the most challenging and will stretch you in ways you never thought possible. Stick it out, the tipping point will come and you will be able to start outsourcing and getting more help along your journey from others as your book success manifests the financial resources to get that extra boost you will need.

It's time to simply Shut Up and Sell Your First Book!

PART 1

48 Strategies to Market Your Way to Success

SECTION 1
PRE-LAUNCH SUCCESS

The sale of your book begins even before you start writing it. After all, if you want to get return on your investment in publishing your book, why wouldn't you start nice and early? There is an opportunity of three months before publication where you can execute your pre-launch and start gaining momentum and a hungry crowd waiting for your book release.

Your pre-launch initiatives make the process feel much more real and your commitment to your timeline you announce is a lot firmer. Don't wait for everything to line up and be ready. Start before you write. Follow the actions outlined in the first five strategies and start getting noticed and offered opportunities, way before your book is in hand.

Strategy 1:
The Power of a Mock-Up Cover

One of the very first things that we do for our authors is help them create a mock-up cover for their book. There are a few reasons for this. The first reason is that it makes the writing of the book become very real. It encourages the author to take those first steps and get the book writing project started immediately. Last night, as I was watching a show on Netflix with my boys, I came up with the idea of this book. Immediately, I messaged my designer and within 10 minutes we came up with the cover. I have already written *Shut Up and Write Your First Book*, so I knew that I wanted the exact same cover except with a different background colour.

Two hours later I was already writing the introduction. Right now, it's the next morning and I'm starting each of the strategies that I want to share as part of this book. I have also contacted my authors to contribute their own unique strategies that have helped them gain leverage and sell more books. I have requested testimonials that I can add into the full manuscript as further credibility for the book and myself. You will find these at the start and end of this book.

Creating a mock-up cover does not need to be hard. On the freelancing website Fiverr, you can hire a graphic designer to design a mock-up cover for just $5USD. Some of my authors have even used the free platform Canva and designed something themselves. Please note that these authors have had a very clear vision for their cover and some designs skills or an eye for it. I personally would not attempt it myself.

Best advice I can give you is to look up various covers on Amazon and see what you like. Choose 3–5 and communicate this with the designer you hire as to what you like and don't like. They will design something (sometimes 3–4 options) and show you. You can then go back and forward with them to share feedback and further ideas until you get the exact look you are after. Once the mock-up cover is done, ask the designer to give you some scenes for your book. See below a few that our designer has done for our authors:

Your mock-up cover may not end up being your final cover. You may completely change it or tweak it as you see fit, right up to the point that you go to print with your book. Even then, it's not too late. You can always change your book cover later to freshen up the look and simply re-upload it with the new cover next time you plan to print. Your mock-up cover will play a big part in your pre-launch campaign, both online and offline.

Strategy 2: Laminate Your Way to Success

Now that you have a mock-up cover, it is time to print it. Either go to your local stationary store or if you have a colour printer and laminator, do it at home. Print off 3–5 copies of your mock-up cover and laminate them. Plaster a few around your house especially where you write, so that you have a constant reminder of your vision and the fact that this 2D piece of paper will soon be a physical book in your hands.

The last laminated mock-up cover you are going to place in your bag to carry around everywhere you go. Don't be shy. From this day forward you are to start introducing yourself as a 'soon to be published author of (insert your book name here)'. This will help drive some pre-sales for your book, so be ready to start taking in those orders. Have an order form printed people can fill out and/or an online way to process a pre-sale on your mobile device. And remember to carry cash change just in case.

The best thing that I see my authors get when they start introducing themselves with their laminated mock-up cover isn't the pre-sales of books, but the massive opportunities they get as a result of the perception they create when they introduce themselves. On so many occasions they have called me up to tell me that they were invited to speak because people learned about their upcoming book, or they developed a collaborative relationship with someone and even picked up paying clients for their business due to the greater credibility this gave them on the day.

This small, super easy to do strategy is so powerful. Do not underestimate the fact it is very basic and dismiss doing it. At the very least this is one that anyone can and should do. The best bit is it will cost a couple of dollars. The return on investment however can be massive. I have found myself following up authors not yet published for their manuscripts and being told that because they picked up so many new clients and opportunities due to the laminated mock-up cover they have had to put the writing on the back burner until they service the business they got just from the mock-up.

Strategy 3: Start Selling as You are Writing

Many authors think that the job of marketing and selling their book begins once the book comes out. This could not be further from the truth. One of the most powerful strategies to build a hungry crowd, build awareness around your book and generate early sales that help you with the publishing costs of the book is when you commit to running a 12-week pre-launch campaign.

We talked about the creation of a mock-up cover, laminating it and carrying it everywhere you go. Now it's time to take an extra step and put a plan in place that will continue letting people know that you are writing, where in the writing journey you are at and give those early adopters the opportunity to pre-purchase a copy of your upcoming book at a lower price point. There are a few things to consider and to create in order for your pre-launch campaign to end up being a success:

1. Setting up a website landing page where you will sell your book. We will go into detail about this in the next strategy.
2. Ensuring all your social media accounts are set up correctly and your book features on them.
3. Picking a day you will do a collection of value adding videos about your content from the book.
4. Writing social media posts, blogs, articles and emails that will be drip fed throughout the 12-week period.
5. Scheduling your plan in your calendar so that you remain consistent.

This is the bare minimum – others have engaged collaborative partners, cross promotion strategies and paid advertising to pre-launch their books. If you are fairly new and don't have a large network or cashflow, this may not be possible for you right now.

Let's stick to the ones everyone can do and should do. I have taught the pre-launch campaign since day 1 to all my authors who attend my retreats and the one thing I have noticed is that less than 3% ever follow through to do a pre-launch campaign effectively or at all. So why is this? Mindset! It all comes back to that. They may do a few posts or a video here and there and then give up as they don't get much traction, sales or response for their efforts.

The thing is that this is completely normal. Anyone that has built a huge following or succeeded with their book or business, had to start at the same place – the place where all you hear are crickets. That should not discourage you; in fact, you should be encouraged knowing that you have begun your journey to building a name for yourself, your book and your future.

Consistency is the main ingredient to success. A 12-week pre-launch campaign and beyond must contain this ingredient. Here is how you achieve this:

Open up your calendar and choose which day of the week you are going to release a valuable post, article, video or even do a live stream about your book content. For example:

Monday – Do a live stream on Chapter 1 content
Tuesday – Email your database
Wednesday – Social media posts on Facebook, LinkedIn, Instagram
Thursday – YouTube video release
Friday – Share something to celebrate about your book writing journey

In the content you will be releasing each and every single week, you are looking to add value and share hot tips, insights, strategies and stories from your book. Please don't ever think people won't buy your book if you reveal your best information from it. They will. This is such a limiting way to look at the value behind your passion. People want to see value first before they will part with their cash. They want to feel like they are getting to know you, the author. In sales there is a famous saying – people buy people. That is the key to any sales and marketing success. Abundance of information and sharing is what is common amongst the most famous speakers and entrepreneurs.

At the end of the day, the pre-launch campaign is more about building like, know and trust with those that end up following you, over how many units of books you end up selling. Let me ask you this: would you rather sell 100 books at $20 or at the end of the 12 weeks be approached by a few potential prospects that become your clients in your packages that could be anywhere between $5–$10K in revenue? I know which one I'd rather.

The book starts the conversation, it is you that ends up being able to add more value and continue to serve people through your expertise or story.

Bonus tip when pre-launching:
Aside from lowering the price of your book during the pre-launch period, you can also choose to encourage more sales with some clever extra things you can offer your early adopters. Here are some ideas:

- Choose a charity that you will donate $2–$5 from each book sold during the pre-launch period
- Everyone that buys during pre-launch will receive a bonus ebook PDF immediately that you can create easily with some relevant information that adds value

- Promise those that pre-purchase your book a personally signed copy from you
- Offer a special 'Chat with the Author' depending on what your book is about. Some coaches offer a 30-minute session which can eventuate in a high value client at the end of it.

Strategy 4: Landing Pages that Sell

The best and easiest way for others to do business with us is by being able to find or be directed to a landing page. It is what will present you and your book in a professional manner and something that you can build upon as you grow on this journey. A landing page is a single page website with just one purpose: to get the visitor to take one action, in this case, to buy your book. If you are not tech savvy, I don't recommend you trying to work something like this out. You can hire wonderful web designers on the freelancing platform Upwork who can get the job done inexpensively. The key part that you play is in what you send them as your instructions and the images and content you supply. Here is what I recommend that you put on your landing page:

1. The cover of your book
2. A photo of you
3. The blurb from the back of the book
4. A short about the author section
5. A short video of you speaking about the book for 1–3 minutes
6. Buy now button and shopping cart integration
7. Any testimonials/reviews you may have collected so far on you or the book
8. Extra bonus set up: opt-in area where you collect visitors details if they choose not to buy your book. Instead they

can leave their name and email and receive something that is complimentary alongside the book as well as updates on the book release. You will need this to end up being integrated with a Customer Relationship Manager (CRM) such as MailChimp.

Your instructions to the website designer may include:
- Colour preferences
- Font preferences
- Any branding if you are in business
- Your URL (the address that people type in to get to your website) I recommend buying yourbookname.com and yourfullname.com
- The hosting details for your website – this you can purchase from where you purchase the URL and then the designer will need those login details to set it all up for you
- Your payment button code if you plan to offer a PayPal checkout as your way or being paid. Otherwise, some designers may help you with a different type of shopping cart options such as using Stripe or something unique to you. PayPal by far is the easiest to set up.

The important thing when you have a website is to have the ability to make small edits to it yourself. So, before you hire someone for the job, ask if they will give you the backend login and password, so that you can do simple edits yourself without having to bother them. Often if you don't have this, each time you want to make a small change, you have to contact them and it will cost you more each time.

Doing it Yourself

I've seen some great websites created by some of our authors. Some platforms to consider if you want to give this a go are:

- Strikingly.com
- Wix.com
- SquareSpace.com

I would create a landing page for a book as soon as the mock-up cover is ready. Don't wait, as you want to have the greatest chance of promoting and showing off your book as early as possible. A landing page with professional, clean and well written website copy can do exactly that.

Strategy 5: International Distribution Made Easy

The world of self-publishing has well and truly taken over when it comes to bringing a book out into the marketplace. Authors have greater control over what they publish and it is ten times faster than the traditional publishing route. Traditional publishers usually take 2–3 years to complete and release a book, whereas self-publishing that has been done well takes only three months overall. Authors don't even need to start with large quantities of books if they don't want to. The power of platforms such as IngramSpark has taken the hard work and expense out of printing and distribution.

I highly recommend that you consider uploading your book through IngramSpark. They are a print on demand company as well as an international distributor with a distribution network of 39,000 online resellers. They take the hard work out of your book being found pretty much anywhere on the internet via the most frequently used online resellers. Amazon, Apple, Booktopia, Barnes & Noble, Fishpond are amongst the most recognised in their distribution network. The best thing is, when the author sells a book via one of these resellers, IngramSpark will fulfil and deliver that order.

Once a month they release a report to each of their authors to advise them how many books were sold and where in the world. Ninety days later, the author will get their commission paid out into their nominated bank account. The royalty is around 20–30% on average from what the book sold for. This is pretty good, when you consider traditional publishers only give their authors 5–15% at the most.

The convenience of IngramSpark is also that you can print your own books and fulfil your own orders to readers that buy directly from you. This is especially important when people in other countries buy your book. IngramSpark has locations in the US, Australia, Europe and UK, which means if someone buys your book internationally, all you have to do is select the closest IngramSpark location to the purchaser and pay for the printing and freight there. If you sold your book for $25, the order may be only around $12.50, which means you are now in profit 50%. I love using this function as it's so convenient. My assistant can fulfil those orders and they arrive at the customer's end way faster than if they were sent from my local post office. The other thing I used to use them for was to order books for myself ahead of time so they meet me at locations I would host workshops or do speaking gigs. After all, books are super heavy and you don't want to be packing them in your suitcase.

The last thing I am going to mention about IngramSpark is not to hold your breath and think that this is going to be the solution to all your book marketing and sales challenges. Don't put your feet up just yet. People still need to find out about your book and you are still the best person to tell them about it. It's fantastic that you can be found online whenever people search for you and your book title. That is the magic of IngramSpark – it gets you found, makes your book and you more credible and those extra sales you will make from time to time are that extra cherry on top.

Having an IngramSpark account does not cost anything – they purely make their money from the printing side of their business and the book sales they fulfil on your behalf. To upload a title is often free and you can easily revise your cover and content if need be for a small fee in the future.

SECTION 2

BOOK IN HAND

Phew!!! Your book has arrived. What is the most important thing to do first? Where do you start? What is going to happen next? These are some of the questions my authors have for me when they finally realise their publishing dream. Up until this point their minds have been with the editing, layout and proofing stages of their books. It's been them and their books. Some of them may have been so engrossed in the book publishing process that they may have forgotten about the pre-launch campaign.

These next strategies will outline what you should be doing first when it comes to getting your book out there. Don't skip steps, do these first and then progress to the later sections.

Strategy 6: Give it Away – What?

What did you say? No way! I worked so hard to write this book, paid money to have it published and now you are telling me to just give it away? I can hear what you are thinking. I agree that all of that is true, but the power of strategically giving away some copies of your book, can propel you to greater success in the future. You have to be clever about it. Think about who you know (your network) and who others know (their network).

The media or people in the media have massive networks: readers, listeners and connections to other influential people. If you want to have greater exposure, it makes perfect sense to send them out some of your books. They will often request this before offering you an interview or an opportunity.

People of influence – nowadays referred to as 'Influencers' – didn't necessarily get to where they are through the traditional media route, but rather via social media. They have worked really hard to build their own following and fans and these people can be an even bigger gold mine for sales of your book. If you end up being promoted by them, their fans have huge trust with them and will generally try out most things the influencer talks about and recommends. The key here is to ensure that the influencer is a good match for the message that you share. You may not know any, or perhaps you do but you have no relationship with them. It's not easy to get on their radar, but offering them to test drive your book for free is certainly a great place to start. Other people of influence can be those simply with large networks as they have built those the old-fashioned way through years of networking, progressing in their career and simply being helpful to other people.

Potential clients – I am going to pose the same question as I did in an earlier strategy: Would you rather sell 100 books at $20 or give away one book that cost you $5 to produce to a potential client that may take up one of your packages that range anywhere between $5–$10K in revenue? But, I hear you think, how do I know this person will become a client? Well you don't. And that is okay, because if you have a strong feeling they are a hot potential, then it's likely that in every 10 of those who you give a book to ($50 in cost) there is bound to be at least one big sale of $5–$10K. Don't hesitate – even when hot prospects don't become paying clients, they usually become raving fans. Fans that talk about you to others with whom you have built greater rapport with by giving them your book.

At the very least, you can consider giving away your ebook version of your book for free. I do this all the time. The first book in this trilogy is *Shut up and Write Your First Book* and that is the one that I give away as an ebook for free 9 out of 10 times. It makes sense, as I really want to educate my budding authors about what is preventing them from stepping up to write their first book. It is only then that they will listen to strategy, marketing and sales. This is where I can help, but in order to do that I must first help them get over themselves. Ebooks are also a fantastic way to generate leads that become part of your world where you add value, send more information and build relationships over a longer period of time.

Strategy 7: Door Prize Power

This has to be one of the most cost-effective ways to get noticed with your book, and to build your network and establish new opportunities. From the time you get your book in hand you should always carry a box of books in the boot of your car and a couple in your handbag or briefcase. You just never know when you will run into opportunities and people that will benefit from knowing you or knowing of you.

Every time I walk into a new event I've never been to before, I look out for a way to get noticed by the organiser of that event. After all they are the one that will most likely know everyone there and are the person of influence in this instance. I would go and introduce myself and see how I can contribute and add value to that person and event. In the case of being an author, you have got your book as the most powerful way to get noticed so what you can do is offer it to the organiser as a door prize. Most events have door prizes for the attendees that get drawn at the end of the event as something fun and a reason for people to stick around.

By giving your book to the organiser you build rapport quickly with someone that has never met you and the relationship begins on a warmer note. When the time comes for the door prize to be drawn, in some cases the organiser may also call you up to the front so you can let the people know what you have donated and what it is all about. If this happens it is really great exposure, as those that are interested in what you have written about will come and chat to you after the formal part of the event ends and who knows, there may be some hot prospects or further book sales from that.

The second thing that can easily happen is that the organiser may end up inviting you to speak at that event in a few months' time. This is a big score, as in a few months' time you will have the opportunity to add more value through an official time slot and being the keynote speaker for this event. The opportunities from this could be even greater. You may pick up another speaking opportunity from someone there watching you speak, you may have hot prospects wanting to enquire further about your book or other ways you help people, you might generate book sales or even meet someone that may end up being a great collaborative partner in the future.

As you can see, a $5 cost can turn into massive next steps and greater exposure for you and your book. The more of these that you can generate, the closer you will get to massive rewards and success. Bottom line is, use your book to generate attention and get noticed. There are always ways to subtly let others know about what you do and your passion.

Strategy 8: Use Your Trade Table

Now that you have a book, you are no longer selling 'hot air'. You have something that people can see, touch and read. With that comes the ability to put together an awesome display trade table with a branded banner, table cloth and other book marketing collateral. The best bit is that wherever you go, not just expos or markets, but running your own events and in other places you speak, you can set up your trade table and this is the place all those important conversations happen with potential buyers of your book. People are always curious to check out what is on sale and will browse trade tables for hours.

Expos – these are powerful places you can meet a ton of your ideal readers/clients. It is best to choose to be part of an expo where these ideal people will go to hang out. There is no point in buying a stall at the Pregnancy and Baby Expo if your book is on finance and law. If your book is on toilet training toddlers, then this is the perfect place to be seen. There have been many books written on how to successfully take part in an expo, so I won't share too much detail here. Here are a few of my best tips:

- Have a special expo price for your book and look to how you can bundle it with something else
- Have a way of engaging people as they walk past – competitions or questions are the ones that work really well to build your contact list

- Make your stand really stand out so people can't help but stop and at least have a look – bright colours, lights and fun at the stand
- Focus on lead generation – always have a way to collect names, emails and mobile numbers
- Network with other stand owners as they are most likely your best collaborative partners for the future
- Look for opportunities to speak at the expo – this will get you noticed even more.

Local Markets – getting known in your local community is important when you are starting out. These options are also inexpensive when compared to taking part in a big expo. Yes, the traffic will be a lot less, but building rapport with the locals can be a powerful way to expand your network and gain word of mouth referrals. Also, local people like to support local authors so take advantage of that opportunity. The same rules apply as at expos on how to set up and engage people – it is just likely to be on a smaller scale.

Strategy 9: Bundle It

There are so many ways to creatively sell your book. Packaging and bundling is one of the best ways to do it. It is also leveraged and much more profitable. We all love to get a great deal when buying something. If that thing is then packaged up with other goodies that are relevant, then it is perceived as being even better value.

For years I have been bundling my book with my event tickets. Everyone that arrives and pays for a ticket for my event gets a copy of my book signed by me personally at the registration desk. This way they also remember me for longer and have something to learn from after the event.

Sometimes you can bundle multiple items in a package. One of my authors Francesca Moi, bundles both her books, a wall planner and ticket to her next event for $97. The value is perceived as massive and she sells so many of these bundles when she speaks at events.

Think about what is relevant to the book and complimentary to the content, that would make for a great bundle. Make sure you can explain it clearly and if online create nice images using Canva to show it off. Over time you may get new ideas and ways of bundling your book with other offers.

For any of your paying clients, include your book as part of their package and as I said earlier give it away to a hot prospect that shows great interest in working with you.

Practise packaging and bundling in everything that you offer in your business. This is what turns your offers into 'No Brainers'. This is what will increase your sales and conversion rate. Before you know it, you will be ordering more boxes of books as you will run out much quicker than if selling your books one by one on their own.

Strategy 10: VIP

The previous strategy I used for many years, but over the last two years I have tweaked my approach by offering a VIP upgrade for my events. Including this upgrade option means there is a lower general admission price point alongside a VIP package that includes one of my books and a few other electronically delivered bonuses. This strategy is fantastic as it really crystalises who is really serious when they come to your event. You will find that your VIPs will be the ones that progress with you to the next steps.

VIP upgrades should also be a bundle of items that create that 'No Brainer' feeling. Test and measure what gets you results – and as an extra bonus tip, remember to offer your VIP upgrade when you start your event to people arriving, in case they want to reconsider getting the upgrade. We find that a handful of people always do. If you don't ask and offer the answer will always be 'No'.

VIP status makes the client feel extra special and they end up being the envy of others who are not a VIP. How do I know this? People have told me and I can see how they respond when they see what the VIPs get. In our live events our VIPs also get front of room sitting which makes them feel extra special.

There are many ways you can use the VIP option – not just in low-cost options but also for high end programs. Here is an example of how we present our VIP offer at our event:

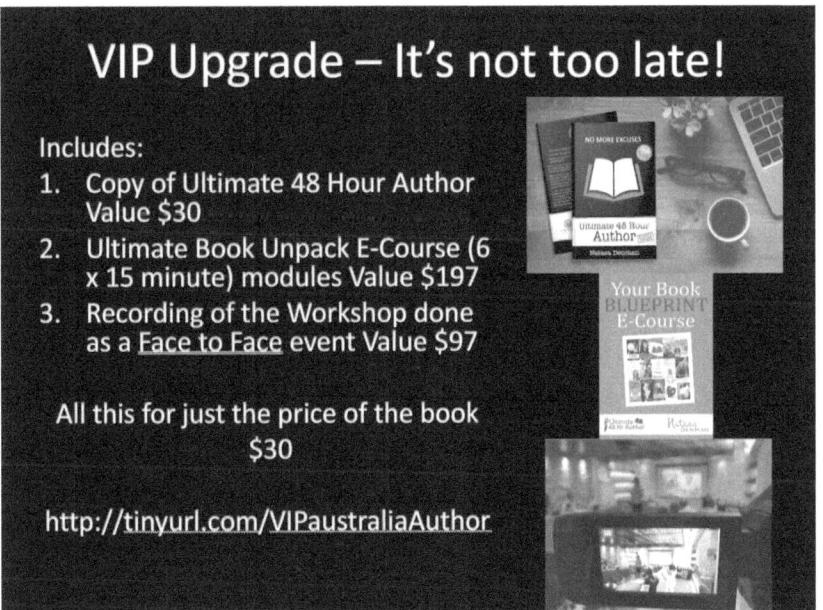

Strategy 11: Get Social Proof

It's one thing for you to say how awesome your book and message are and another when others give their opinion on it. Yes, I am talking about collecting reviews and testimonials for your book. People like to see, hear and read about what others think of a book before they make a buying decision. In the early days when your book just gets released this is even more important. Asking for reviews and testimonials should be happening consistently and indefinitely. You always want to have current reviews and testimonials. My suggestion is to work out a system for this so that it's easy to replicate and you can outsource it to an assistant in time.

There are a few different ways to get reviews and/or testimonials:

- Put a note in all your books you post out to kindly request a review once the person has finished reading the book. You can put your email address on there so they can action it easily.
- If you know some of your readers have bought your book on Amazon, then they can leave a review there.
- Goodreads is also a platform where books can be reviewed without having had to purchase the book as you would on Amazon.
- You can request that someone leaves you a recommendation on your LinkedIn profile or on the Facebook Fan Page for the book.
- Request a video testimonial from those that know you well and would be willing to go that extra mile to do that for you – they are great to put on your book sales page.

How to use reviews

Aside from reviews showing up on your Amazon, LinkedIn and Facebook accounts you can also use them in other areas such as:

- After your email signature (keep them very short here – just one-liners)
- On your book website sales page and overall website
- On unique social media posts – use Canva and include the review with an image of your book
- During any speaking engagements on your presentation slides
- On any marketing collateral – such as banners, flyers, business cards, brochures, etc.

Don't get disheartened if you don't get one from everyone you ask!!! People have good intentions but don't always follow through on their promises. Here are some tips on being successful at getting them to follow through:

- When asking, think about offering something of value to them in return for their time and effort in doing it for you – it can be a checklist, PDF or resource they would appreciate
- If possible always specify the return date you need it by
- Follow-up two days after the return date if it hasn't come through
- Follow-up twice and then leave it alone – you don't want to be seen as a stalker
- Have a thank you email ready for when you get one. Show your appreciation for them taking the time to help you out.

A final word on reviews and testimonials: if you want them to focus on a certain aspect, feel free to ask for that. You can always ask for a testimonial to be tweaked and edited. Most people would be happy to oblige. You can even write a suggested one for people and send it to them for approval. This works really great for super busy people. Don't stop asking for them when you get 10–20. Keep going and keep them fresh – that is what will continue selling books and building your profile and credibility.

SECTION 3

HI-TOUCH SUCCESS
(OFFLINE EXPOSURE & POWER)

It's time to pound the pavement. This is not easy, but it is totally worth it. It is also the fastest way to get known and sell books to people. Offline exposure is the first place you will establish yourself as an author and win your readers over with your passion for your story and/or expertise.

The following strategies share all the offline opportunities you must execute to build your network and generate the like, know and trust feeling with them. These strategies take time, effort and consistency. They will be the foundation to everything you later will be doing online and the starting point of your message gaining momentum and spreading – first nationally and then internationally.

Strategy 12: Local Library Launch

Local libraries love supporting their local authors. They are also willing to put on a launch at no cost for authors. When starting out you may not have massive funds to put on your own book launch, so you can contact your local library and introduce yourself. They often look for ways to add more value to the community and are proud of having authors that live local to them. If you do get an opportunity to do this, please don't simply rely on their promotions of the launch. If you want it to be a great success, look for ways that you can also spread the word and get people there on your big day.

In addition to that, ensure that all your marketing material, trade table, banner and intention for the book launch are set. Work together with the library staff responsible for putting on the launch to come up with a strategy and plan for the time you have there. Remember to donate a few of your books to the library so they can be lent out. You never know who may read your book, be inspired and reach out.

The key mindset here needs to be that you are getting greater exposure within your local community, more people find out that you and your book exist, and you are practising how to speak in front of groups. No brand-new authors started with massive book signings and book tours and were invited to simply be at a venue because they wrote a book. Authors that get these opportunities have been around a while, started exactly where you are, and now they have the credibility that opens up doors to lucrative marketing opportunities.

Being successful at authoring is no different than achieving success in any other endeavour. No-one sees the small things you put so much effort to do and the times you only had a few people at events.

This is where most will give up which is really sad. The tipping point is available to all those that commit and stay on the journey. Do the work, pay the price and then you shall reap the freedom and choice that a comes with being a successful author.

Strategy 13: Put on Your Own Party

Hosting your own book launch can really take things to the next level. You can choose the venue, food, drinks and really think through the set up and run of the night. Organising a professional photographer and videographer will allow you to capture great photos and video that you can use for promotions on your website and social media. You may also be able to seek out sponsors for your book launch which can help cover a lot if not all of the costs. Those that are complimentary to what you do and not in competition with you may want exposure to the people that would be in attendance. The media often will run a piece on a local book launch so don't forget to contact them.

The purpose of a book launch is to make the release of your book official and celebrate the hard work you have put in. It's also a form of publicity that will attract more people to check you out, hopefully buy the book or maybe even want to discuss being a client and working with you if your book is related to your business.

Another way to cover almost all the costs of a book launch is to have a ticketed event. I have done this many times for all the group book launches I have hosted for my authors over the years. Here is our book launch system that you may like to get some ideas from and maybe model. I have removed some specific logistics from it and left the bits that are relevant to you.

The intention for a book launch should always be more about being seen, building brand awareness and generating leads. Book sales do happen, but they are not the main focus of the night.

Book launches can be free or ticketed. We have tried both, and found the paid launches were the most successful. Not only did this approach guarantee our numbers, we also saw an increase in the number of books sold on the night. If you break it down, a $30 ticket (which is generally the price of a book) covers food on the night, a drink on arrival and a copy of the book for each guest to take home. This is great value.

With three weeks to go, organise a three-email sequence to invite people on your database. Schedule one to send three weeks out, then 15 days out and then five days out from the launch. Posting an event on social media and keeping people updated is also key to getting more attendees.

During the last 10 days, I suggest sharing the launch via your social media channels more frequently, saying how excited you are, and putting the registration details in the comments field. Make sure you really let people know what they will be getting for the $30 – especially a copy of your book on the night and an awesome networking opportunity.

One week to go buy your supplies and get ready. Here is a checklist of what you need to bring along so everything runs smoothly:

- Copies of your books (work out the number according to how many tickets you have sold and add 20 extra on top)
- Tablecloth for your table. Be creative with the colour, match it to the book and remember you can buy a flat sheet if you can't find a tablecloth

- Anything you may like to put on the table like an inspirational word, eye-catching props or sprinkles. I buy some stars from a craft shop to dress it up even more
- Vertical banner (if you have one) to put behind/beside your table
- Pen for signing, in your favourite colour if you like (I always choose pink)
- Clipboard to keep your paperwork together
- Any prizes you will give away as a door prize
- Cash change and receipt book for cash payments
- A way to take credit card payments – most use PayPal or Square attachment to their phones
- A well-prepared speech.

Here is another checklist to help you to remember to organise all the important things that will make it a successful night:

- Where will you hold it? When choosing a venue, it should be central to most areas with ample parking available
- How you will set it up? Choose decorations that match your book theme
- Will you run videos and need audio? For events with over 40 people in attendance you will need a microphone and speaker
- Will you hire a professional photographer or videographer or both?
- What times will the food come out?
- Who will help you on the night? You'll need extra people on the door for registration and to help with logistics
- Have you communicated the registration process to your crew?
- Have you organised some door prizes from you and sponsors?
- Will you have an MC?

- Will you have sponsors and other speakers?
- How will you structure your speech? Will you be interviewed or make a speech?
- What will you do about music for the night?
- Have you organised your drink and book vouchers?
- Have you pre-signed the message in your books so you only need to personalise them to save time?
- Have you sent out your logistics emails before the launch? Don't forget to send out a follow-up/thank you email after the event too.

On the big day, plan to arrive at the venue two hours before the event so you are set up with one hour to go and can relax and have a drink. Change into your good clothes once set up is all done, and take flats with you if you are a girl that may wear high heels for the official part of the night.

Don't avoid or bypass this strategy especially if it's your first book. It's a great experience in coordinating an event and the exposure can really propel you and your book forward. Also remember, you can have multiple book launches in different cities if you choose. My authors normally live interstate so they do one in their home city and then come along to take part in the group book launch one with us. Most of all, really enjoy your special night – those memories will stay with you forever.

Strategy 14: Bundle Packages for Special Times of the Year

Throughout the year there are special dates and holidays that we celebrate – from Valentine's Day, Mother's Day and Father's Day, to country specific holidays or even religion specific ones. Your book topic may fit in line with one of those and linking it up to the holiday can really boost your sales. The media loves to run content that aligns with holidays and would be more willing to give you coverage if you are linking up your value that way. It's a clever way to get noticed and stay relevant.

We have spoken earlier in the strategies about bundling and packaging and this is now also the perfect time to do exactly that. Each holiday generally has gifts specific to it and with some of those bundled with your book it can make for a great package for people to buy. Using this strategy, you can sell more books and make extra money if you create a package that is greater than just a book sale. An example of this is when one of my authors, Moana Robinson, bundled her book *B Styled for Life – Living with Sass and Style over 50* with some of her services as a package she offered a month before Mother's Day. This was a great idea and she sold quite a few of these bundles. The best thing was, people have subsequently hired her to be their stylist and have worked with her at a high-end package – a lot higher than a $30 book sale.

How can your book be linked to a special holiday in the year? Get creative and really think about it. It may not come to you immediately, but be patient and think about it from a few different angles. Once you come up with the idea, test it out when the time comes around.

Strategy 15: Network, Network, Network

If I had to start all over again, this is what I would do every single time. The power of networking and real time and place relationships fast tracks the success of any business. In this case if you have a book and you are selling it, you do have a business even if you don't think you do. The more people you connect with, the more people that will find out that you exist and what your message is.

When I started out, I was told the best way to find clients was to get out there networking and attend two events every week. I made this my 'rule of thumb' and got started. After the first 12 months I had attended 104 networking events. As my first book arrived at month 13, the relationships that I had established over the previous 12 months really paid off. I got asked to speak at people's businesses now that I had a book, I got referred more frequently as my networking buddies had a way of speaking about me and passing on my book to those that needed help. Collaborations were also coming my way from the established relationships. I always tell my authors to start with this strategy way before they get their book in hand.

So how does one go about networking with others? There have been many books purely written on this topic alone, so I recommend that you pick up a few to read in detail. Here I will give you a few tips and pointers that will get you started.

Finding events

A lot of people just starting out have never heard of networking. Networking is actually everywhere. When we go to parties we network, when we play sport we are connecting, and when we talk to someone new, we are becoming known to them.

In the world of business there are more formal ways of networking which are called business networking events. The purpose is to meet like-minded people, build the relationships and ultimately see how you may be able to assist or refer one another. Networking is not about going to find your next client at the next event. It may happen occasionally, but this is not the purpose that you should be walking into an event for.

Once you decide that you will get out there and network, I am sure event options will start to show up everywhere. There are many offline and online events happening all of the time. So, which one is right for you? That is hard to answer and decide unless you go and try out a few different groups. As you test out the waters in different groups, you will see what feels good and the type of format you like. Some networking events are more male dominated, others are female only and some allow only one category per type of business to be a member.

If you don't know how to find them, a question post on social media to your current network or in a business group will help. You may end up with way more options than you thought. Once you find a few that you like, I recommend becoming a member with them, so that you turn up regularly to all of the meetings and really get the relationship building under way. Most groups will have an annual fee and maybe even per event fee (for food or drinks). Investing is important as it locks in your commitment to the group and the fact you will be a valuable member that contributes to its success.

Before you go to any event, set your intention. Is it to connect with a new specific business you need help from, is it to meet a potential collaborative partner or is it to simply do great in your pitch? This is the time given to each person to introduce themselves in the group. Not every event does this, but the majority do.

Here is a helpful template that can help you craft yours:

Your BBQ Speech/Pitch
The absolute secret to being able to gain a prospective client's interest quickly is to appear valuable to them, to appear as though you may be able to get them something that they want.

To achieve that end, you need to develop your BBQ speech which you will use when introducing yourself or when asked what you do (as might happen at a BBQ, or at a brief business encounter). To have that, you need first to have clear and concise answers to the following five questions:

A. With whom do you seek to do business?

_____

_____

_____

_____

B. What are their 3 biggest and most critical problems?

1. _____

2. _____

3. _____

C. How do you solve those problems – uniquely?

_____

_____

_____

_____

D. Include a client's most dramatic (WOW!) results.

_____

_____

_____

E. List the deepest benefits your clients gain & how they feel about those.

_____

_____

_____

Now let's put together your BBQ Speech, which will always take the following form:

1. You know how (answer to A.) do, are or feel (answer to B.)?
2. Well, what I do is (answer to C.)
3. The result is (answer to D.)
4. The benefits are (lots of answer E.)
Let's try that:

You know how

_____

_____

HI-TOUCH SUCCESS (OFFLINE EXPOSURE & POWER)

do, are or feel

_____

_____

Well, what I do is

_____

_____

The result is

_____

_____

One of my recent clients

_____

_____

_____

_____

_____

An example
You know how a lot of business owners find themselves overloaded with work and people issues and, often, with tight cashflow, and can feel stressed and on the edge of control a lot of the time? Well, I use some really simple systems to lower their workload, improve their leadership, free up their cashflow and create new profits. You'd be amazed at how much different those clients look and how differently they feel after just six months.

One of my recent clients who, with 32 staff was still generating 60% of her company's sales has changed all of that. Last week she came back from a three-week cruise and told me that she was training her staff for her five-week cruise starting next month. Sales are up, profits are up – and she's no longer responsible for any sales. She looks about 10 years younger, and reckons she feels that too.

Putting your BBQ Speech into practice
Rehearse this until it's totally natural and you'll be fascinating to everyone, and of huge interest to the right people, or to anyone who knows and cares about people who would benefit from making your acquaintance.

Once you have your hook into their 'interest nerve' turn on your *Active Listening*, ask lots of questions about *them*, and you're going to look like the most interesting genius they've met this year! Your social challenges are over!

At the event
Now that you have your pitch sorted, it is time to go along to the event. It is important to arrive on time or slightly early. Don't be too early as you will distract the organisers while they are setting up the venue. Perhaps park and sit in your car and then arrive exactly

on time. Arriving on time, allows you to settle in and start talking first to those that are also there on time. Informal networking is usually where the opportunities arise, and you can determine with your fellow networkers how and when you will follow-up on what you discussed. This normally happens before the event starts and after the official schedule finishes for the formal part of the event.

When starting out, it can feel really awkward showing up at events where you know no-one. It feels scary and unfamiliar, but most people that network always look to engage a new participant, so they don't feel alone. The key is to make a deep connection with just a few people and not try to get to everyone. This is impossible and makes you look desperate. Also don't hand out business cards unless you are asked first, or everyone has them in a box or on a table to look through. I always like to think of myself as a 'business card collector' rather than giver. The reason for this is because when I collect business cards, the ball is in my court to follow-up with that person after. People are really bad at following-up and this is their biggest shortcoming. It also makes networking a waste of time. The secret is in the follow-up and the long-term relationships that you develop.

Networking is not a magic bullet – it is a slow burn process that gives back in truck loads as you do it over a long period of time. It starts off being awkward and nerve-racking but becomes fun, exciting and a great way to connect with others especially if you are starting out alone on this journey. Don't forget to keep showing up at the same events as the repetition of people seeing you is where the like, know and trust is built.

Follow-up
The work is not over when you leave a networking event. It actually has just begun. Ensure that you connect with those you met on social

media and send them a nice message and/or email to say how nice it was to meet them. Do not sell ever in this follow-up! Talk about something you may have discussed during the event and be easy and casual in the communication. Follow-up with those that you may have said you will meet 1–1 online or offline and lock in that date and time immediately. I follow-up within 24 hours of an event while people still remember me and what we spoke about is fresh in their minds. If you wait any longer, you may as well not do it. Follow what your contacts are doing online, comment on their posts and share in turn what you do, by sharing valuable posts and content. As people follow each other over time, they reach out when the time is right to either buy from you or you buy from them. If you are not going to do the follow-up, don't bother networking – you will waste a ton of time and money.

Strategy 16: Speaker Bio Secrets that Get You the Gigs

Nine out of ten authors want to speak as a result of writing their book. They have dreams of sharing their message or story and inspiring others. This is fantastic, but where they get stuck is how to find and get those speaking gigs that will enable them to do exactly that.

Creating a speaker bio is one of the easiest things and I recommend it to all my authors. I ask them to create one, put in the back of their books where the offers are and also print it out on nice glossy paper to carry around wherever they go just in case the opportunity comes up to share it with someone. I also tell them to store it as a PDF on their computer for easy access if they want to apply to organisations or events that are looking for speakers online. The sad reality is, less than half will put in the effort to pull this one

HI-TOUCH SUCCESS (OFFLINE EXPOSURE & POWER)

pager together. Here I will show you mine and a few examples of author speaker bios and then walk you through what you need to have on yours in order to go ahead and create one.

Natasa Denman is The Ultimate 48 Hour Author. A highly sought after professional speaker (CSP accredited - Certified Speaking Professional), Natasa is a 7 times published author and creator of the game changing business model, Ultimate 48 Hour Author. She has helped over 150 small business owners become first time published authors in just 3 years.

In 6 short years in business, Natasa has been nominated for The Telstra Businesswoman of the Year twice and was a finalist in AusMumpreneur of the Year in Product Innovation.

Appearing in all major media outlets across Australia, Natasa is changing the way people do business in Australia and now runs a 7-figure business with her husband and 3 children travelling the country, spreading her message and helping small businesses thrive.

Ultimate 48 Hour Author Blueprint for Business Success
- How to Leverage Your Business via a Book
- Lucratively Position Your Book for Success
- How to write a book in Just 48 Hours

Ultimate Brand Accelerator Formula
- How to Stand out and Thrive in Your Industry
- Hi-Touch, Hi-Tech and Hi-Fame Strategies
- The One thing that will Fast Track Your Following

1000 Days to a Million Dollar Coaching Business from Home
- How to build infrastructure for a 7 figure business
- Marketing Smarts to keep your Pipeline full
- Sales Mastery Insider Tactics

 +61 412 085 160 | natasa@natasadenman.com | www.natasadenman.com

FAYE READ

Faye is a Registered Midwife, Prenatal & Childbirth Educator, Energy Intuitive, Author and International Presenter. She is passionate about empowering women and their partners to have a positive birth experience. Faye is equally passionate about creating change in the landscape of birth across the globe. Her business **Peaceful Pregnancy** is a partner organisation with 'Birthing the New Humanity'...Birthing the change.

Sharing over 30 years experience in Midwifery and private practice as an Energy Intuitive and Natural Therapist, Faye has helped hundreds of women and their partners to achieve a Conscious Conception and heal previous birth trauma, supporting them to go on and experience positive birth outcomes.

As an engaging and inspiring speaker, Faye brings to life the journey of the Soul... emerging through the portal of birth and crossing the threshold to new parenthood. Her spiritual insight, paired with her grounding in Midwifery offers a new perspective on various topics:

Overcoming the Fear and Trauma of Childbirth
- Understanding the nature of fear, pain and trauma and HOW to overcome it
- Prenatal Imprints and Spiritual perspectives of pregnancy and birth
- Tools of empowerment for positive birth

Feng Shui Tips to Put the CHI Back Into Birth
- Ancient wisdom...modern day practise
- Creating Sacred Space for a conscious conception and birth
- Empowered birth = empowered parents

Voices From the Womb
- Conscious Conception
- Communicating with your unborn child
- Partnering with your baby at birth...it's all about THEM!

Contact Faye if you would like her to speak at your next event.

📞 **0417 471 526**

@ faye@peacefulpregnancy.com   www.peacefulpregnancy.com   www.whatimpregnantagain.com

Your speaker bio gives organisers a clear picture of who you are, what you can speak on and what the audience will learn as a result of listening to you. It is also important you have this designed professionally, so that you can print it off and give it to those who are looking for speakers. There are five key aspects to think about when creating your speaker bio:

1. Your sexy/hypnotic personal bio
2. Your sexy/hypnotic keynote topics (3 in total)
3. Your sexy/hypnotic takeaway points (3 per topic)
4. Your credibility images
5. Your contact details

Here is a template for you to fill out to start pulling all of this together.

SPEAKER BIO TEMPLATE

Rewrite your About the Author bio down to 100–120 words. Use the best and most credible parts of what you have achieved thus far. You are looking to present a star profile. Use my examples earlier as a guide. Don't be shy. Let yourself shine!

Sexy/hypnotic keynote topics:

1. _____

2. _____

3. _____

HI-TOUCH SUCCESS (OFFLINE EXPOSURE & POWER)

Sexy/hypnotic takeaway points for each keynote topic:

TOPIC 1: _____

- _____
- _____
- _____
- _____

TOPIC 2: _____

- _____
- _____
- _____
- _____

TOPIC 3: _____

- _____
- _____
- _____
- _____

Credibility images you will use in the design of your speaker bio:

- ☐ Professional photo of you
- ☐ Your logo
- ☐ You speaking in front of an audience if you have it (if not add later when you do)
- ☐ Your book cover
- ☐ Media logos if you have them (if not add later when you do).

You do not need all of the above, just what you can come up with. Ensure they are in high resolution. Once done with the above send all the details to a designer to pull together your awesome speaker bio. Update your bio every 1–2 years or more frequently if things are changing for you especially in the early years of speaking. Put your speaker bio amongst the offers at the back of the book, print it off on nice glossy paper and keep the PDF of it easily accessible on your computer.

Always remember to carry it around and listen and look out for opportunities to speak. Research online by googling 'speaker callouts (YEAR)' for a particular year, you may be able to also apply for certain opportunities and speak at conferences all over the world. If you have been doing the networking I was suggesting previously, the warm relationships you have built with those people should start opening up opportunities to at least present and speak at those events. Most networking events always have a guest speaker that covers off a certain topic for the group. These are the best ones to start with and work your way up from there. Your speaking here generally won't be paid but they will allow you to set up a table with your banner and books and have the opportunity to make an offer at the end of your talk. At the very least you will sell some books to the audience.

This particular skill is scary to think about developing, but if you do and put yourself out there, the opportunities magnify as you are exposing your message one to many and in the case of face-to-face events, people love getting their hands on the product after the event.

Don't avoid creating a speaker bio especially if you want to speak. It is the one thing that will differentiate you from other wannabe speakers who say they want to speak but have nothing to show for it. Go in prepared and make the organiser's life easy so that they choose to give you the gig.

Strategy 17: Handbag & Boot

Your book is your business card on steroids. You put in time, effort and money into bringing it to life so please don't hide it away. I see this in many authors who shy away about showing their book to people and in events. They omit putting it on their website or if they do, it is in some hidden area no-one can find. I know as I have visited some of their websites and wondered where the book is. I say, splatter it over every single page, make it part of the template the website uses for each of its pages. Don't make it hard for people to find.

But this strategy is not about your website. This one could not be simpler and easier to do. From the time you get your book in hand, put a couple in your handbag and a box in the boot of your car. There have been so many random situations where I have been asked for my book at events while I have chatted to strangers as the conversation led to a point where I showed them my book and they were interested in getting a copy. As I carry the second one in my bag, I would sell them that one and if I ever got stuck, I would say come and meet me at my car after the event and I can grab you one from my boot.

You just never know who you will meet and speak to when you are out and about. Don't miss out on these random opportunities to make book sales. Also make it part of how you introduce yourself and look for ways to talk about being an author and the book you have written. If you are passionate about your topic and message this shouldn't be hard as it will come through you naturally and with energy and enthusiasm.

Strategy 18: Get Some Press (Press Releases to Media)

Being in the media completes your rockstar profile. A rockstar profile portrays you as an author, speaker and a person in the media. Make sure that you promote those three things when being introduced, via social media or on your website and your speaker bio. Once you have been featured in the media, those logos (as seen on) will be yours for life. So how does one get media coverage?

As an author it should be easier. The media is looking for those with credible authority which is what authorship gives you. The most important thing to remember is the fact that the media is not interested in your book, but the **'issue behind the book'**. By addressing this in your press releases, you will have a huge chance to get those call backs and be featured in articles, magazines, blogs, radio and even TV. The best thing is that this publicity is free yet worth thousands.

Some of my authors really tap into this strategy big time. They do a great job and then get reinvited for further exposure in the future or become regular contributors to a media outlet. From this I see them sell lots of their books and services as the book ultimately gets mentioned at the end of an article or somewhere during the interview. People look them up and reach out for more information. In addition to that, the appearance on media can be featured on their website, the logo of the media outlet can be put on their profile and the longevity of this exposure stays with that author forever.

There are some key things to ensure you get right if you want to approach the media. First of all, start small and work your way up to bigger media outlets. Find out which are relevant and have your ideal audience that would want to hear about the issue you speak on. Sometimes this may not be the mainstream shows, but it could be industry magazines or particular niched blogs. They will want to know that you know about them and who their readers, listeners or viewers are.

Next is to learn how to properly write a press release. There is a particular very stringent format that all media are used to and if you want to get a look in, you must follow it. Press releases are written in the third person and laid out in a specific way. Take the time to learn from someone how to write one correctly. After you have written it, it is time to send it in via email to the journalist. If you cannot locate their contact details online, phone the media outlet and they will share this information with you.

After you email it, one of two things will happen. You will get a call back very quickly (which is really uncommon) or you will need to follow-up 24 hours later with the journalist. The latter is pretty much what you would need to do every single time. It is important not to ring at an inconvenient time otherwise your call won't be taken. If you are calling to get the details for the contact person, you may want to ask when the best time is to reach out for a follow-up call.

When you get the journalist on the phone for your follow-up, they may not have seen your press release. Have your emails open and immediately resend it to them that moment so they can scan through and give you a yes or no answer. After all they get sent hundreds of press releases every day and their inboxes are super full all the time. Don't be afraid to ask why not if they say no to you. That way you can take that feedback on board and try again next month. It is important to be persistent to build a relationship with journalists. A good rule of thumb is to submit one press release per month per media outlet before you become a pest.

This strategy when you learn how to write a press release, send it in and follow-up, can be a powerful way to keep being seen and remain top of mind with people with your message and book. If you focus on it for 24 hours each month, your media opportunities can skyrocket your book sales. I encourage you to do some further reading on what journalists want, how to write press releases and uncover where your greatest opportunities for media lie. I went to a 3-day seminar in my first couple of years of becoming an author which helped greatly with our success in the media.

A word on PR agencies
Hiring a PR agency to do the work on your behalf is an alternative way to be featured in the media. This is great if you have the funds to invest in something like this. What you must be mindful of is the return on investment. How many books would you need to sell to get the return on investment for the services you are paying for? Is it worth it? Do they have some kind of guarantee? You need to weigh up what is important to you.

I worked with a publicist who was not part of an agency and specialised in helping authors get more media. His rates were not as high as an agency would charge and I decided to take a risk to invest in this experience. It actually turned out great. He got us a lot of article and blog opportunities, some mainstream newspapers and lots of radio gigs. For what we invested it was totally worth it to build our credibility further and show this off on social media, our website and my speaker bio. I rehired him a further two times which also worked out great. His services where a three-monthly engagement. Do your research well if you are considering something like this, contact people or get referred to those that have a great reputation in this field before you give away your hard-earned cash to PR agencies that may not produce any results for you.

Strategy 19: Run Your Own Events

For the last decade I have been hosting my own events where I get to meet new people who find out about me, my books and the business. I get the opportunity to add value with information after which I offer the audience a few options of further learning. This can be by buying a book, online program or working closely with me via our retreats and one on one programs. This works the same way for every niche. I did it for weight loss with my first book exactly the same way.

If you do decide to run your own events, my suggestion is to have more on offer than just your book. It takes a lot of time, effort and money to pull together and execute your own events and even if every single person in the room buys your book, you will never come out in profit. In fact, you will most likely lose money. Events are the most powerful when you have a high-end offer that helps people with implementation of the information you share and then the books sit at the back of the room for purchase is case some of the people really like what you have said but are not ready to take the next step or really can't afford it at the present time. This way, buying at least the book is a way of them learning more and staying connected with you. By running events, I was able to leverage my time one to many and grow first to a multiple six figure business and now a multiple seven figure business. They truly are everything I do nowadays. For authors, I think this is the most profitable strategy.

The 'how to' of running events is way too big a topic to cover here but I did write two full books on exactly how to do it a few years back. They are called *Bums on Seats* and *Fully Booked Retreats*. Those books really break down the whole process behind how to promote, prepare and profit from events and retreats. Here I will give you the five things you must get right when starting out to run your own events:

1. Your Event Title and Blurb – what will people get out of coming along to your event? This can really make or break your success in attracting the right audience. Keep testing it until you find one that speaks out to the exact people you want to attract. Using your book title sometimes may work and other times it may not. Be mindful to use hypnotic works and state the outcome in the title.
2. Lead up time – when organising an event, it's important to have a good lead up time for promotions. A face-to-face event needs at least 4–6 weeks of lead up to get a good number of bums on seats. For high-end events you will most likely run smaller events that sell into them so that lead up can be 6–12 months.
3. Promotion of your event – there are many free ways to promote your event, but they will take a lot of your time. I talk about those strategies in the book *Bums on Seats*. Then there are paid ways like Facebook Ads, Instagram, Google Ads etc., where you spend more money but less time in getting new people to find out about you and register for your event. Unless you are really confident in exactly what you will be able to sell when you speak in front of 30 people (your conversion rate) and you have a product/program that is proven, paid ads can be a huge risky investment. For the first five years in business, I did all of the organic strategies to get bums on seats and then I invested in ads. Nowadays, with confidence

I invest more than six figures in ads which I know will eventuate in over seven figures in sales. Don't skip steps and don't give up too early.

4. Turn up no matter what – I have a saying: you never cancel or delay an event. No matter how many people have registered or not registered, you turn up and do your thing. There have been many times I would turn up to rooms with five or less people and once even one person. I still delivered and got business from these events. Another thing I say is to never underestimate the size of the group. In smaller groups you can build deeper rapport with your audience and get to know them better and therefore you achieve higher conversion than in rooms with 50 or more people. Always turn up, always do your best and keep tweaking your presentation and calls to action as you learn from each event.

5. Document your results – write down after each event exactly what happened. These are the things I write down:
    - How many people came
    - How many were 'no shows'
    - How many and which books did I sell
    - How many bought my high-end program
    - What were all my expenses like venue hire, promotional expenses, travel, accommodation, flights, car hire, etc.
    - What was the total revenue from the event.

These numbers are super important as you do more and more events. You will be able to see how you are performing over time as an average. There will be peaks and troughs along the way. Don't give up when you have a few crappy events as the snowball of good stuff is most likely just around the corner.

When running your own events, you take the full responsibility – but end up with the greatest power! You can have whatever call to action you like and do it exactly the way you feel it should be done. As you take the full responsibility and risk, the rewards are the highest. It's not easy, but totally worth it. People following you will further perceive you as an expert, and as you host events, your credibility will skyrocket as they now see you in a leadership position.

Strategy 20: Influencers

If you want to fast-track your journey to success and gain massive exposure, but you don't have a network yourself, there is a way to achieve this a different way quicker. The key is to find those that do have large networks and followers that will help out. Nowadays we call them influencers or people of influence. They have spent the time engaging their audience and built the like, know and trust with them. So, if they recommend something to their followers (like say your book) then you are likely to get a lot of sales in the process. After all, it's a lot more powerful when other people say your book is awesome than when you say it yourself. Getting publicity for your book also works in the same way.

This strategy makes sense but it's not easy to do. However, if you think about it this way then your time spent doing this will pay off. Rather than spending time nurturing relationships with those that do not have large networks, how about doing that with those that do. To notice who has a large network or following here are some key tips:

- Are they the event organiser? Event organisers know a lot of people and generally will have a database.
- Are they a speaker? Speakers usually connect with people one to many and gain a lot of exposure.

- Look up the person on social media – do they post often, how many followers do they have and what are the reactions and comments on their posts like?
- Google them – if they are active and lots comes up on Google then this is also a good sign.

To get closer to a person with a large network my best tip is to see how you can help them first. Do not even think that you are simply nurturing this relationship to get something for yourself. It has to be genuine and to the point of developing a friendship. When people become this close, they end up doing stuff for one another. You will know when the time is right for it to feel like you can ask.

In my experience for example, I turned up to events a bit earlier to see if I can help out with setting up the room. I also stayed to the end and offered to help pack up anything. This gave me an opportunity to talk to the organiser and speaker when no-one was there. The more times I regularly turned up, the more we connected and ended up catching up outside of the event.

On social media, I would comment and exchange banter with them on posts and after a while, reach out and see if I could connect to work out if there was a way I could help them. On any one to ones I looked for a way to be helpful and do something for them. As this progressed, we reached a friendship level that felt like we could ask anything from one another. In turn, they were more than happy to promote my events and books. I also offered my book as a door prize at many events which made the organiser look good and in turn gave my book exposure.

It does take time to do this. The best time to start was yesterday. The next best time is today. Write a list of the people you know that have large networks and a following and make a goal that you would like to get closer to three of them over the next year. By setting the intention you will bring it into reality.

Strategy 21: What's Your Number?

For anything in life we really want, we must set a goal for. Selling books is one of those things you can quantify and if you want to sell a certain number over a certain time, then set a goal for it and break it down. What I have learnt about goals over time is that we are actually not after the goal, but rather the feeling we get from achieving it. Here is some brief information and a template on how I write and think about my goals. I encourage you to do this for various areas of your life. I write my yearly and 90-day goals consistently and on time, every 90 days. They are diarised and it happens like clockwork.

There is a lot of evidence and research that has proven the amazing benefits of goal setting. People that set goals are in the tiny minority of the general population – and they are also that tiny minority of people that experience abundance in many different areas of their lives.

In fact, a study of Yale University graduates showed that only 3–5% of all students set goals. These graduates were followed through life and a measure of their net worth was used as the measuring stick as to who experienced the best results later on in life. What was found after 20 years was that the 3–5% of the graduates that set goals actually had a combined net worth more than the other 95–97% that did not set goals. Something to think about …

Similar research on goals set around health, weight loss, relationships and personal development has also shown that the people who have set those goals reach them – and in most cases, exceed them.

If you were to book a trip for a holiday, what is it that you need to do first? Know where you want to go. You cannot just walk into a travel agent and say: 'I want to go on a holiday, please book me in.' Even though the travel agent will give you some suggestions and ask you a few questions around what an ideal holiday for you is, you still must decide where to go. This is your End in Mind – The Destination! Think about your book sales destination for the first 90 days and/or one year from the time when your book comes out. Or, if it's already out, for the time ahead.

When you have your destination, the steps to get there make up the action plan of how you will make this happen. For a holiday you would need to take the steps of booking flights, accommodation, travel insurance, organise your travel documents, any vaccinations you may need, pack for the trip and figure out how you will get to the airport on the day. For a book it would be many of the strategies you have read through thus far.

To arrive at your destination, you will need to take the actions necessary to fulfill the previous steps leading up to you being there. That's the easy part as often people find it hard to think big enough when setting goals.

If you Believe you can achieve a certain Goal, You are right!
If you Believe you cannot achieve a certain Goal, You are right again!

The importance of goal setting
If you are anything like me, I love getting from A to B in the fastest way possible. I know most people do. We all want to get rich quick, lose weight overnight and have instant gratification around food or materialistic items. We continue to look for that magic pill and quick fix that so much of today's marketing promises. And guess

what – we buy into it. We believe such a thing exists and pretend not to know that it truly doesn't.

If there ever was a magic bullet to getting the wheels in motion, goal setting is it. If you can see it, imagine it, put language to it and write it out as a commitment to yourself – I know for a fact you can manifest it. The power of goal setting is seriously underestimated by the majority of the population – in fact 95% of the population. Why?

Familiarity. Goal setting has become so familiar and common that almost everyone takes it for granted. Familiarity keeps you stuck, motionless to take action and change your circumstances.

Let me share a couple of examples …

Can you remember a time when you first met your partner or the start of a new relationship? I do. I know we all go out of our way to impress the other person. There is touching, listening, talking and doing things for one another. It's all exciting and new. Such an amazing time to look back on. So, what happened? Why aren't you experiencing those joyful times today or ongoing?

The answer is you became comfortable and familiar to each other. Everything that needs to be said has been said, everything that needs to be explored has been explored and the commitment is there so why work at it any longer? He/she is not likely to run away. You became comfortable and familiar to the point that you stopped growing together and stretching your relationship to new levels and points of discovery. You are now bored and stuck. There are two possible roads you will take: stay in the relationship, set some goals and get to work or leave and repeat the same pattern with someone new. I like to think of familiarity as the killer of our dreams and potential.

Another example that everyone can relate to is in the workplace or business. A new job or venture is exciting at the start. It challenges you and you often find yourself thinking of the future possibilities. As the months and years pass by, you can find yourself in one of two places. One is excited and challenged by it because you are always stretching and learning to master your craft to new levels; the other is bored and unsatisfied. The latter also happens due to familiarity.

And what about your health and wellbeing? Why do you think people stay overweight and unhealthy? Familiarity once again. The state their body is in has become so familiar, so comfortable and changing behaviour and actions around this is often viewed as too hard. The little voice in their heads keeps banging on about will it work for me, what if it doesn't work and every other excuse imaginable comes up so change is avoided at all cost.

That is why people don't set goals. Because they are so familiar with the concept and setting goals means that they will actually have to move and take action to achieve them. They will have to get uncomfortable, go into unfamiliar territory. Arghh, pain – the stronger of the two motivating forces: pain and pleasure. We do more to avoid pain then to experience pleasure.

What happens when you goal set?
There are three key things that occur when you set goals:

1. Tension in your brain
2. Commitment
3. Ownership

Tension in your brain – you create this with the sheer fact that you are not where you want to be. This tension is good, if not great. It moves you to action. It makes you feel uncomfortable and motivated to get to where you have said you want to go. Use it to your advantage and you will achieve amazing results going forward.

Commitment – setting pen to paper is super powerful. The sheer fact that you are writing down what you want to achieve engages a couple of your senses. Visually you can see your goal in front of you and kinaesthetically you feel yourself committing it to paper. Also reading your goals out loud and with conviction engages the auditory sense – a great way to add more oomph to the power of goal setting.

Ownership – your end in mind is different to everyone else's. You are unique and your standards are just that – your own. So do take responsibility for your results and set what you want, not what others want for you. Goal setting creates the feeling of being in charge of your destiny. Choose not to drift but decide what will happen and how you will see it to reality.

Change is by Choice, NOT by Chance ...

What is goal setting?

Goal setting is a series of paragraphs and commitments you make to yourself around certain achievements you want to see real in your life. These should include all areas of life not just health or career. I encourage you to divide your goals into five key areas:

1. Health/Wellness
2. Personal Development
3. Business/Career
4. Family/Relationships
5. Financial/Materialistic

Goal setting is all about stretching yourself to experience new levels of success, abundance and growth in all areas of your life. After all, if you are not growing what is happening instead? One of my favourite sayings is:

You are either Green and Growing or Ripe and Rotting.

People that have lived the longest lives filled with abundance and happiness are those that have stretched and set new levels of achievement for themselves, even post retirement.

I watched a video recently where Tony Robbins interviews a 108-year-old woman that is still self-sufficient, lives in a one-bedroom flat in London and continues to practise at her piano three hours per day. She survived the holocaust and the concentration camps during World War II with her young five-year-old son at that time.

I learnt a lot from this 12-minute video. I learnt that she looked at everything as a gift in life (even the concentration camp experience), I learnt she was thankful for everything and had a picture in her mind of survival and life post war. She focused on giving and mastering her craft of being a brilliant pianist. She still continues to do this even though today may be her last day. She wrote a book at the age of 105 and the thing I most loved was that she said: 'I know about the bad, but I choose to look at the good.' Wow!

So, let's look at the good and see where you want to be …

How to goal set
Goal setting is not as simple as writing out a one liner, although this is better than not doing anything at all. I am here to teach you the right way to set goals, so that you can set yourself up for success easier and get there faster.

When you set goals, you are influencing your subconscious mind to take action and get you to your destination on autopilot. Before you start thinking that all you have to do is set those goals and they will magically manifest in your life, I am here to tell you until goal setting becomes an ongoing habit that is mastered on a regular basis this won't be the case.

It takes effort, focus and action to turn your goals into reality. The best goals to set are 90-day goals. This time frame is long enough to accomplish a significant task or project, but short enough that it creates that time pressure for you to take action. I wrote my first book because of a 90-day goal I set. And the best thing was, I had it done in 80 days.

Next are your one-year goals. These will be either an extension to your 90-day goals or new bigger goals that may take a whole year to complete. For example, a personal development goal for yourself may be to read one book per month in the first 90 days and the extension of that translates to 12 books in one year or you can create a stretch whereby you may say 15 books for the full year.

All of your goals must be written:

- Using the SMART Template (described below)
- In the Present Tense
- 'As If' you are already in possession of them

S.M.A.R.T

The SMART model is the most widely used way of making sure your goals are set the right way. Each letter of the acronym stands for something different and there has been a few different versions of what each letter stands for.

S stands for SPECIFIC – a specific goal has more chance of being accomplished than a general one. The more specific the better. For example: I would like to be fitter. A more specific example of this would be: I will swim twice a week and go to the gym three times per week. To make this section of goal setting easier you could ask yourself the following questions:

1. Who: Who is involved?
2. What: What do I want to accomplish?
3. Where: Identify a location.
4. When: Establish a time frame.
5. Which: Identify requirements and constraints.
6. Why: Specific reasons, purpose or benefits of accomplishing the goal.

M stands for MEASURABLE – when you set measurable goals you have the ability to know when you have achieved them and if it has been within the time frame set out.

They keep you focused on the how much or how many. It also helps to ask yourself the question: 'How will I know when I have achieved my goals?'

A stands for ATTAINABLE – in setting goals that are important to you, you tend to start focusing on how you can make them come true. You start looking for alternatives on reaching a particular goal and you are more open to other opportunities that may not have been obvious to you earlier.

All goals are attainable if you break them down into smaller steps and work out a wise time frame that allows you to carry out those steps. They start appearing more within reach as you grow and expand to match them. You see yourself as worthy of these goals and you start developing the attitude, traits and personality that will allow you to possess them.

R stands for REALISTIC – in this part of goal setting you need to ask yourself: Do I really believe I can achieve this goal? Often setting more difficult goals is better because you get to have more motivational drive in achieving them. In saying that though, having a goal that is far out of reach may demotivate you since your belief in attaining it may not exist. It is great to stretch yourself and set your goals more frequently, so that you get the feeling of being successful and you start building reference points for success. This will build your self-belief in achieving bigger future goals.

T stands for TIMELY or TANGIBLE – the first thing I would start with in goal setting is this part. Having the date adds that sense of urgency to a goal and it sets your subconscious mind into motion to begin working on that goal.

Finally, a goal is tangible when you can experience it with one of your senses. Those are touch, taste, smell, sight or hearing. The three most common senses I would describe my goals in are to ask myself to describe: What am I a going to hear, see and feel when I achieve this goal? This makes the goal tangible, and it has a better chance of making it even more specific and measurable.

Now that you have the criteria for setting goals, I would like to take you through how you would go about writing out a goal and an example of a perfectly composed goal that you can model to write out all of yours.

HI-TOUCH SUCCESS (OFFLINE EXPOSURE & POWER)

Example:
It is 30 March 2022, and I have sold over 1000 books. By going out networking, running one event per fortnight and being a guest speaker at other people's events once a month, my credibility has climbed to the next level. I feel proud of my achievements, I see people buying my books from my website and at live events and I hear amazing feedback on the book's content from my readers.

Here is a template to fill in:

It is _____, and I have _____
_____
_____
_____
_____

I feel _____

I hear _____

I see _____
_____.

Setting rewards

Setting rewards as a result of achieving a goal is a powerful way to keep yourself motivated. Some may be small rewards and others bigger – it's up to you to gauge and decide how you will set those. The two key motivators for change are pain and pleasure. This takes care of the pleasure side of the equation. Even if you don't hit your exact number, I always like to say I achieved that goal 70% or 85%, which is a lot more than if I never set it or attempted it.

Strategy 22: Multiple Book Launches

Having met and helped so many first-time authors, I have noticed that their belief is that they can only have one launch party near the release of their book. This is not true in case you were thinking the same! You can launch your book whenever you like and as many times as you like. While I am writing this book, we are living through the coronavirus pandemic. Events are pretty much non-existent and no-one really knows when they will be happening again. However, books are still being written and coming out. Some authors have attempted online launches which is better than doing nothing at all. This doesn't mean they cannot host a proper face-to-face launch when things change and we can run events.

Another thing to think about is launching in different locations. Plan a tour of different cities where you will put on a launch. One thing to be mindful of is that in other cities you may not have a large network of those that will come along to support you. So, you need to treat those as events that you will need to hustle to get bums on seats. Perhaps getting some publicity in the local paper from that area, posting the event on places like Eventbrite and contacting some independent bookstores that may be interested in having an author signing at their location may help with foot traffic.

I want you to remember that travelling and launching isn't just about selling books. It's about meeting people and building an awareness that you and your book exist. Some conversations with those you meet can lead to other opportunities that you didn't even consider. It's great PR for your book, you and your brand. If you have a business behind the book, then you may even connect with people that will hire you to work with them.

Remember to take lots of photos and videos, and post it on social media, so you get the leverage online by building the perception of being out there. This itself may draw your online followers in closer checking out your activities and being further inspired. Every action that you take may seem to reap small or no rewards in the early days, but I want you to remember that all of this works like compound interest. You don't see huge rewards till much later on – and when you do it's like a snowball effect. The only thing is that it cannot be predicted when the snowball will come.

Strategy 23: Meet the Author

I already mentioned in the earlier strategy about contacting independent bookstores to see if they would have you in for an author signing. This works great for those that may not feel confident pulling off a launch party by themselves and it would also attract a different audience and people you have never met that normally shop in that bookstore.

Let me break this down a bit more for you if you want to try it out. When approaching a bookstore, you must walk in with a win-win outcome. It can't be just about you and the fact you are an author. It has to be beneficial to that business and its customers. Look at that bookstore's flavour (are they spiritual, children's, business or a bit of all genres). Figure out who the decision maker is and go and introduce yourself. You may not ask the first time you meet them. I suggest ask some exploratory questions like:

- Do you do author signings here or meet the author days?
- If yes, how does all that work?
- How do you get books for your bookstore? Is it via distributors or do you sometimes work directly with the author?

- Do you have percentage range of royalty that you give to an author when their book sells in the store?
- How do you process returns if books don't sell?

You can even pretend you are learning currently to understand a bit more how something like working directly with a bookstore may look like. Tell them you are new at this and doing some research and whatever they are happy to share would be super helpful. They may even give you more information beyond the answers to the above questions. It is only through asking that you will gain the wisdom to cater your approach.

When the time comes, contact multiple bookstores with your win-win outcome to have you on site for a day. Make sure that you make their life easy, ask what you can and can't do as you are on their turf and want to respect the opportunity they are giving you. Assure them that you will have a professional set up and display so that it matches the ambiance of their store. Get your pull up banner made, think about the dress up of your display table and also how you will get people's contact details, so you stay in touch beyond the day. Remember after the day, to send a follow-up message to those you connected with and send some flowers as a thank you to the bookstore for having you. Doing it this way, you are saving money and having foot traffic that you didn't work or pay for.

Strategy 24: Book Distributors Revealed ...

In order to get your book into the chain bookstores, you will need an official book distributor. Being in mainstream bookstores will give you more credibility over being a massive money-making strategy. Think about your reasons why you may take this path. I personally never have as I like to have full control over my books. For some people it's an ego boost and nothing more than that.

For others they do want to work with the distributor and drive sales everywhere.

Getting a traditional book distributor still means that you will be responsible for creating your own publicity and media hype in order to get people buying your book from stores. Book buyers (the stores) are not guaranteed to stock your book after the book distributor rep has been to see them, and you will only be getting 30% commission of sales less costs. Woodslane is one of the industry leaders in Australia that offers book distribution. Others would work in similar ways.

After reviewing a contract, we extracted some key points to be aware of when it comes to working with a book distributor:

- The book distributor requires exclusivity to the market (online retailers such as Booktopia, bookshops, library suppliers) – this may mean you will have to cancel your own account with other online resellers like IngramSpark or Amazon Create Space. I would ask this question
- The book distributor charges an admin set up fee of $350 and a title listing page fee of $30 per title per year
- They also chare storage fees of $6.00 per m3 or $500 kg, whichever is the highest
- Costs for returns of misbounds and remainders will be charged back to the publisher. This is you, as you are self-publishing
- Costs of pulping @ 10c per item
- Extra advertising costs for inclusion in sales catalogues
- Stock on hand – would be 12 weeks supply (**they offer print on demand also)
- Retention – 20% on termination of agreement until costs are assessed and offset against monies owing (post 90 days).

These are just some of the items noted. I am sure the pluses are your book will be circulated by the book distributor sales rep to the store buyers on your behalf and it has the potential to be sold in the outlets you are looking for. For airport distribution in Australia, you may also like to approach WHSmith directly.

The internet also contains lots of information on book distribution that you may like to educate yourself around, if this is a route you want to try for yourself.

Strategy 25: Niche Businesses

Bookstores are not the only place people buy books. Think about the stationary store kikki.K – they sell a few books on organisation, planning, decluttering. Lorna Jane (the activewear retailer) sells books on health and wellness. My chiropractor sells books on health and wellness but more related to the benefits of chiropractic. I've bought books from these stores myself. I personally had an author signing at my local gym when I was launching *The 7 Ultimate Secrets to Weight Loss*.

Start thinking broader than bookstores. Are there businesses or stores that are within your niche that would benefit from having your product on their shelves or as a recommendation to their customers? Write a list of who they are and start making some introductions. Once again, a reminder to not try to get a deal going immediately. Remember, relationship before requests. The only reason I got the gig at the gym was because for months prior to the book coming out, I got close with the gym owner while networking at a local monthly event. If a business is going to take your book on board, they would really need to align with your values and your content has to align with theirs.

Once again, when putting forward a proposal for such a collaboration, it needs to be win-win. Every time that business sells your book, what do they get and what do you get? Can you refer people you meet their way as you are in a similar niche? Make sure that you are not in competition with one another; the relationship should be complimentary. Check in with them from time to time, take in a professional display that would help them show off the book and ask them how things are going to get feedback if it is working or not.

SECTION 4

HI-TECH SUCCESS
(ONLINE EXPOSURE & POWER)

Digital is the way of the future. It is also the only way you will be able to get known outside of your home city. This is also why I recommend starting local first, as you can then go online and share your local successes, so you can start being noticed by those that are not in your local city.

The power of social media, email, video streaming and so much more are key to an author's success. After all, an author is the key ingredient to the information era we are living in. Authoring is not just about releasing a book. Your responsibility beyond your book extends to you adding value and curating content to further your message. Writing a book alone is simply not enough. Keep reading to find out what I mean in the following strategies.

Strategy 26: Real Time Value

Technology has advanced so fast and we can now connect with our networks and followers in real time. Anyone has access to their own reality show in their pockets via the power of smart phones. Live streaming is the way influencers connect with their followers in real time to add value instantly. This is available to you as well. It may be something that can seem daunting to begin with, but it does become second nature with practice.

If you haven't created your own videos before, I recommend starting there before diving into live streaming. Start with some short 1 to 3-minute recorded videos on your book content. Share stories, tips and key insights from your book. If you need, you can do multiple takes until you get it right, unlike live streaming which is unfolding live and you cannot correct your stuff ups. My recommendation is that you release a video or two per week to grow a following. When you are a bit more comfortable, attempt your first live stream. The key is to be prepared. I often make shorthand notes in the notes section of my iPad or iPhone and when I go live have them open as reminders on the content I wanted to cover. Your content is in your book so all you need to figure out is which part you will share and talk about in more detail.

Please don't think for a moment that people won't buy your book if you reveal parts of it in live streams. People will be even more curious to get the full picture of what is in the book. In today's world, marketing has moved away from being pitchy and salesy to being value driven and educational. If you are not adding value and educating you are missing out on so many sales and opportunities.

Here are some tips on live streaming:

- Plan to be on live for a minimum of 5 minutes or longer – as you want others to realise that you are live and join the stream. This takes a bit of time to generate.
- Ensure you are adding value from the moment you go live as there are many others that will watch the live stream as a recording later – don't be one of those people that sit around and wait for viewers – it looks really silly on the replay.
- Choose a sexy magnetic headline for your live stream – this will get them scrolling to click through and start watching and following.
- Acknowledge those that comment and join the live stream – after all you are there in real time and this will have those people coming back to watch you in the future.
- Do your live streams from interesting places and locations – remember this is your reality show.
- Choose to live stream for 30 minutes a week each week at the same time so that people start noticing you and even scheduling when you will be live. This way your live audience numbers will grow over time and people get used to seeing you at the same time each week.

Remember, you get better and more at ease with repetition and practice. Most will never attempt this strategy and miss out on massive opportunities in real time.

Strategy 27: Read Your Book on Live Stream

This strategy isn't something I have done myself, but quite a few of my authors have done it with great success thus far. Each week or every other day, they would jump on a live stream and read a part of the book – either a story, part of a chapter or even full chapters. So, you may be thinking, won't that stop people from wanting to buy it? Well, the reality is, it is unlikely anyone will be available for the whole time you read out parts of it and really the key is to get as many people as possible to hear you message, story and build greater rapport and closeness with you.

Remember what I said earlier – today's world wants to experience value and education before they commit to making a buying decision and investing in a product or service. Another way you can look at it is that those who are listening to your live streams end up becoming raving fans of your story/message. They quite often will be the spokespeople and your word-of-mouth army that shares how awesome you and your book are. They end up selling it for you as now they will know more about what is in it and who would benefit from it.

When live streaming, create a nice space that others recognise and get familiar with when they see you live. Have a nice and neat background. It is critical to remove distractions and position yourself professionally. If you are a business owner having your branding in the background or a media banner works a treat.

Finally, when live streaming ensure that you have great lighting. Here are the three different types that I love and always use.

Laptop Light

Ring Light

Mobile Phone Light

The ring lights are a little hard to position behind laptops or desktops, but do work well as you can use them if putting your mobile phone in the middle. My favourite is the rectangle light that suctions onto any laptop or desktop and for mobile use the clip attachment light shown above. If you don't have any of this type of lighting, ensure you sit in front of a window so that the natural light hits your face. Never have light behind you as you will look dark in your videos. People don't stay to watch live streams if they are of poor quality.

Strategy 28: Opt-In Power

I am sure you have noticed that most online resellers of books such as Amazon, Barnes & Noble, Booktopia, Fishpond etc., offer you the option of downloading a sample of a book before deciding to purchase it. This is a clever strategy for selling more books. A sample is usually enough for you to decide if you want to keep reading or not. Why not model this same strategy for yourself to capture new leads that you can nurture a relationship with over a period of time? A sample also allows the potential reader to see what is on the contents page for the rest of the book. If you have named your chapters with hypnotic words that entice and create curiosity in your readers, then you are more likely to have them wanting to buy the full book. So, how does one go about this? Here are the steps:

1. First thing you would need is the sample of your book. You can ask your layout designer to give you the book in PDF format, with Chapter 1 and 2 included.
2. Use a 3D image of your book in the area where you will have this call to action.
3. Your website will need a fill in form (also called an 'opt in') so that those who visit can enter their details (name and email is enough) in order to receive the sample.
4. The form will need to be integrated with your CRM (Customer Relationship Management) System. This is where your lead's details are stored and where you can set up the delivery email with the sample of the book. You can also set up automated emails beyond the delivery of your book sample to further add value, nurture a relationship and have more calls to action over time.

This set is not easy to do on your own especially if you don't view yourself as a techie person. It is best to ask your website designer for help in the set up.

Furthermore, you can capture leads from the other online resellers with your sample. The way you do this is by creating a free bonus offer as a lead magnet to capture those leads. In this case, it is not about giving away the start of your book for free as they are already getting that from the online reseller. What you are doing is offering something of value additional to your book that the reader may be interested in downloading. Here are some ideas of what your freebie can be:

- Bonus PDF that is relevant and adds further value to the book
- Templates or checklists
- Take a quiz
- Audio files
- Video files
- Free membership to a community.

You may promote this free offer at the back of your book, however I strongly suggest that you also mention it in the first 10 pages of your book. This is because those that are interested in more information but do not actually buy the full book, may go ahead and download your freebie by following the call to action that appears in your sample. After all, another reason this works amazing is because a lot of people don't finish books, and you want to be able to have them enter your world via your database so that you can be in contact with them over a period of time. What happens is that they will either end up buying something from you in time once you have built enough know, like and trust or they will simply unsubscribe from your database if the information is no longer relevant to them.

Once again, this set up requires some techie skills to put together and it is very similar to the way you would capture leads that want the sample of your book. You may want to choose one or the other, or even better is to have both.

When thinking of your website, make sure that your lead generation opt-in shows up on all pages as people may click around. The key is to make it easy for them to decide to stay in touch with you via your free bonus.

Strategy 29: Create Some Canva Magic

Your book and message don't sit on their own in order to sell. You would have noticed that the book plays a part in all things so far, but there are also many other additional tools you need to create to make the promotion of it a success. Here I would like to introduce you to a wonderful graphic design 'do it yourself' platform called Canva. I've mentioned in a couple of the strategies so far, and when you learn how to utilise it, you will have so much fun creating professional images, promotional flyers, social media posts that pop and pretty much whatever your mind can imagine when it comes to having visually appealing marketing collateral for your business and book.

Canva is free to use, although for some of their stock images you may need to pay a small fee to use. Otherwise, they have plenty of free images, or you can bring your own, upload and simply start creating. They have wonderful templates so that you don't need to be a graphic designer to make things look visually appealing. I use Canva all the time for various things for my business and books when I want something fast and I don't want to wait for my designer to do for me.

In this case I recommend you use Canva to create some beautiful quotes from your book and then you can put your book cover and the website where people can go and get it on the bottom of the image. Here is an example of one of mine.

I use the same template over and over and just change the quote. This makes it recognisable and reusable over and over at different times. I use quotes of what I normally say, not what others have said. You can see all my branding is there, my photo, name, book and website. If someone was inspired by the quote, they may decide to share it (quotes are like that – people share them all the time). As the quote gets shared, those that don't know me yet may end up being curious about what I am all about and check out my website and books in turn. These may be people interested or looking to write a book themselves which are my ideal readers and clients.

Another way to look at this sharing is in the terms of value and being generous with your content and information. By regularly posting fresh new content or parts of what you have written about, it gives people a small taste. They become more aware of you, and when you are consistent, it keeps your book and what you do top of mind. Some of these strategies won't reap you rewards and book sales immediately, but they are all a combination that builds the good will of your brand and message and keeps you in the public eye showing up to share freely and regularly.

If you are worried about using a tool like Canva, don't! It's a simple drag and drop platform and if you spend 5–10 minutes playing with it, you will master it. If you really get stuck just look up a few tutorial videos on YouTube and follow what they teach. But be warned, when you learn how to use it, it can become quite addictive and you will want to create so much with it. It truly is a life changer and a great alternative if you cannot afford a graphic designer for everything you do. I have taught my virtual assistant to use it and she does all sorts of amazing things on it for me.

Strategy 30: The Podcast Circuit

A new form of media has really grown of late and that is podcasts. Anyone is able to start one and some people have had huge success with them. With millions of listeners, they have been able to monetise them further by giving companies that want exposure to their listeners the opportunity to advertise their business on the podcasts' ad space. As an author that wants to sell more books, this is one space you must explore by either getting on the podcast circuit or starting a podcast of your own.

Starting a podcast of your own is the easier of the two if you have the confidence and know-how. If you don't have the confidence, start off by being a guest on other people's podcasts and gain the knowledge from being part of other podcasts, or by reading books or doing a program that teaches you about podcasting.

There is an awesome platform where you can post your podcast for free and they distribute it to all the main platforms. It is called Anchor FM. The way I do my weekly podcast episode is not directly on Anchor FM but I host a weekly Monday morning 'Live with Nat' on my personal Facebook profile which is public. From there my virtual assistant downloads the episode, puts it on my YouTube channel and then extracts just the audio from it and puts that on Anchor FM. This way my weekly content gets spread out in many different places and in different formats. After I finish my Monday morning live, I also write two content rich emails that we schedule to go out to the database on Tuesdays and Thursdays. With one piece of content, I am able to provide value to readers, listeners and viewers. If you want to spread your message far and wide without needing to always be coming up with new content, this is an easy and leveraged way to do it. You just brainstorm your content for the week (I like to do this Sunday afternoon on my iPhone on my Notes app) and then you deliver it Monday and have someone that would share it all over the place for you.

Now let's talk about getting the opportunity to be interviewed on other people's podcasts. Like on traditional media, you may start off with smaller podcast hosts that have smaller followings and build your way towards the larger ones. The best way I have found this works amazing is by being introduced to a podcaster and recommended to be interviewed. Podcasters are always looking for experts and appreciate a recommendation. They usually ask their other guests recommendations to save time on searching for new guests. Some bigger podcasts even have a website where people can fill out a form to recommend someone else.

I remember a few years back, a business colleague of mine asked me if I had ever listened to the podcast 'Entrepreneur on Fire' by John Lee Dumas. I actually had from time to time and so I knew what she was talking about. She then continued to tell me that I should be featured on that podcast. I was very flattered as that podcast has millions of listeners and is very well known. I said to her, I would feel weird applying for it myself and if she wanted me to be on it to go ahead and recommend me. There was a form on their website at the time where you can recommend a guest, so she filled it out. A few days later I was contacted, and the interview happened weeks later and it launched as it happens on my birthday!!! My database skyrocketed that day and I have had people reach out to me many times since, long after that episode aired. That was a big win!

Look out for posts on social media where people look to interview others or even consider being interviewed on Facebook Lives which is an alternative way of getting exposure to someone else's network. On a Live you can even show off your book a few times during the call as you speak and refer to things from your book, you can lift it up and point to it. Visually it is a great way to get people to want to grab it if they found you interesting and want to get the full content. The most important thing is to have somewhere to direct all those listeners or viewers – either your website or a specific landing page where they can grab a free gift. Go prepared and with an intention set of what you want to get out of it – books sales or leads. Have fun and share these interviews in turn on your profile for further exposure and credibility.

Strategy 31: Run Your own Webinars/Online Seminars

An alternative to face-to-face events is to run them online instead. It is the same thing, but it requires better technology know-how and a slightly different approach to the face-to-face model. When the coronavirus pandemic hit in March 2020, after a decade of running events offline, we were forced to move them online overnight. I was so scared. After all I was selling a 20K program and felt that people needed to meet me in real life in order to make a 20K decision to work with me. But a couple of weeks later I was proven wrong. I had over 20 upcoming events that I had to convert online. They were solidly booked and most of the attendees were happy to swap to online as they were in the same situation stuck at home.

The first event was horrible. I really didn't enjoy it, but I learnt a lot of what didn't feel right. I tweaked my presentation for the next one and that was very average too. Still no conversion. I said to myself, I just need to keep doing it as repetition is the mother of all skill. The third event was my USA now online tour and the LA event was first. This was the defining moment when I had a ball hosting it, the group was really fun the way they interacted with me in the chat box and we ended up with seven clients from it. I started to feel like I do in real life events and I was able to get the groups interacting with me by sharing when being taken off mute, watching their faces of how they reacted to what I was saying. I continued to further tweak and refine my presentation as I kept doing more events.

Online events are so much cheaper to run. The only expense you really have is your promotional expenses, the platform you will use for hosting the event and if you invest in a booking system. It is really important to get the technology right and know how to use it efficiently. This is what you will need to master:

- Sharing your screen with your presentation and not sharing your screen
- Remembering to record your event every single time so you can use that to send to those that did not attend
- Managing the chat box (having another team member with you online always helps) and in time you will be able to present and read comments that you can acknowledge as you go along. This all depends how many comments there are and if it's appropriate to say something at the time
- Your call to action – what do people need to do at the end of the seminar. Book a chat, go and buy something – those links need to be at the ready so it is seamless and easy to do.

With online events, the world is your oyster. Because of our transition online, we are actively working with the US and Canada as well as our home market all over Australia (not just the capital cities we could travel to). We were able to reduce our prices slightly as we removed so many hard expenses of flights, accommodation, venue hires, parts of the package and of course the massive amount of time we were on the road to make the face-to-face happen. We even host online retreats now which have proven to be more successful than the real-life ones as our clients can focus better and are more productive and less distracted by the social interactions in a face-to-face retreat. We still have a ton of time and fun, and they get to know each other during and after the retreats.

Finally, the world is way more accustomed to online right now and people of all ages are logging in to be part of an online event. By moving fully online you can be location independent, work with more people worldwide and reduce your costs significantly. Some of the disadvantages are that it's harder to build rapport online, you need to follow-up a lot more with people and they can drop off your call easily leaving you sometimes with a handful at the end. I believe that these can be overcome by being committed to repetition, learning and tweaking every time you do one. When you get the formula right, your life will never be the same again.

Strategy 32: Get Blogging

Writing a book is not the end of your writing days – it is actually the very beginning. Because if you want to sell your book, your message needs to spread in all kinds of ways. Blogging is one of them and it can be a powerful way for people to get a taste of what you are about and you can remind them they can go and get the book from your website in the P.S. of the blog. Blogging is also a great habit to get into as it creates the opportunity to practise discipline especially if you commit to releasing one blog at a particular interval of time.

You can set your blog up to be part of your website and once written you can share it on your social media platforms, convert it into an email for your database or deliver it as a live video (also called a Vlog). Remember, you do not need to be always coming up with all sorts of different content, you can use one piece in many formats and have that as you weekly blast.

You blog may not have many subscribers when you start out so it will take some time to grow. I still recommend you get into the habit of blogging as it is really great for your consistency and discipline of writing. To get greater exposure with your message, consider being a guest blogger on big blog sites like Huffington Post, Mamamia, Moz, Mashable, etc. These blogs get more readership than a lot of media outlets. It's not easy to get on them but it works a very similar way as it does approaching the media.

Some of their websites may have an area to pitch an idea for a blog, so you would go ahead and do that. It's important to check out the niche of the blog first so that you are not wasting your time pitching an idea to something that is unrelated to your message. If you feel that those blogs are too far out of your reach, do your own writing, approach other ones that are not as big as practice for the big guys. If you don't try to skip too many steps, you will always get to where you need to be in time.

Remember that success is available to everyone, but most people perceive successful people as being lucky and only notice them once they have the success. What no-one notices is the early years of hard work, rejections, hustling and non-existent cashflow. If you actually ever take the time to speak to someone you admire, ask them about their first few years when they started out. You will hear a very similar pattern in their story. Working 24/7, learning non-stop, investing in mentors, risking family income, getting rejected all of the time, etc.

A successful author is not one that hides away in a log cabin and sits back counting the dollars in the bank from book sales. They are out there in the world meeting people, connecting online in various ways and keep banging on about their mission with their message. The movies and TV shows portray authors in the light of this secluded freedom they live, but this is not real life. I am not saying that one day you can't do exactly that if you want to, but it won't be when you are just starting out.

After 10 years, I became fully location independent, but I am still really active online and gaining exposure with my message all of the time. Prior to that I hosted/attended two live events every week, consistently. Over the 10 years that is a total of over 1000 events. I would say 500 of those I have attended and/or spoken at and 500 I have self-hosted. I am committed to serving and helping people with my message, story and system. If you make the same commitment, you too can enjoy the fruits of your labour, once you have paid the price.

Strategy 33: YouTube Time

YouTube is a huge social media platform that many avoid due to the fact they are scared to get on camera and speak. Well, I say get over yourself. You have to start somewhere. The only way you get good in front of the camera is by actually getting in front of it. By building you own YouTube channel, over time you will have a great library of resources and content that you can repurpose any way you like. After 10 years I have 1631 videos on my channel at last check. I never set out to even think I would have 100 let alone what it has got to over time. This is because I film everything and put it on there. I film my seminars, Monday morning lives I do on Facebook and any short content videos I create for my niche. It is actually not something I devote time to doing, it kind of happens along the way as part of my weekly commitments and activities.

Here are some important things to remember and do when setting up your YouTube channel:

- Use your name as the account name not the book name
- Create your channel art in Canva and make sure you put your book cover on it. If you don't feel confident doing it yourself hire someone on Fiverr to get it done for you.
- Create your introduction trailer video for your channel to entice visitors to subscribe to your channel
- Enter you contact details in the description next to your introduction trailer (see image of my channel) use the http before your website so it turns into a clickable link

HI-TECH SUCCESS (ONLINE EXPOSURE & POWER)

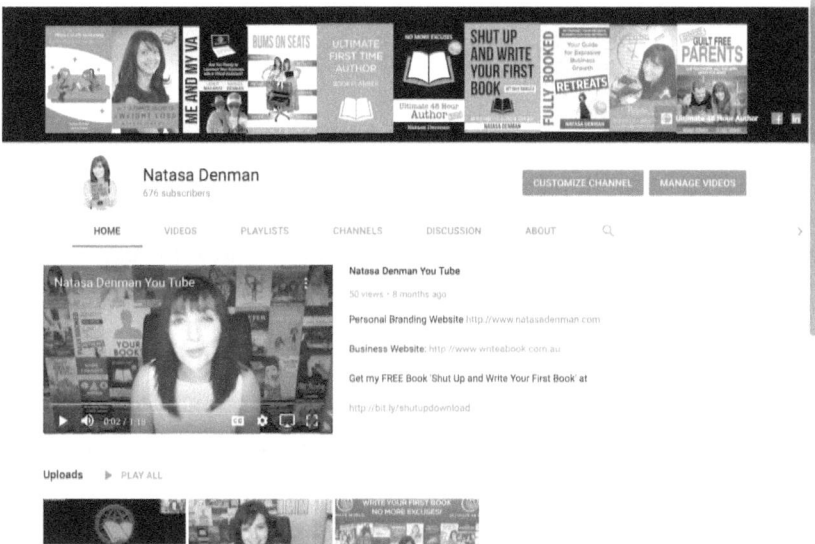

- Put a nice profile photo of yourself
- Use catchy and hypnotic titles for your videos that contain keywords people would search to find the information you share
- In each video's description once again put your website with http first, then describe the video and finish with the http. This way if those watching really enjoy what you are saying they can easily click through and end up on your website for more info. That is where they will find your book and hopefully buy it.

With video, the two most important things are light and audio. Always have the light hitting your face when choosing a position to shoot and ensure either no background noise or use a microphone that will produce great audio. Also think about what you will wear, what you will have in the background of your video and of course start prepared with notes on what you will say being clear in your mind. You can from time to time in your videos have a call to action for your book and even hold it up in some of your videos as you may reference some information from it.

Being natural and at ease comes with time and practice. Once you really own your stuff, you will be doing videos at the drop of a hat and possibly even become what my husband calls me 'A one take wonder'. Happy shooting!!!

Strategy 34: Keep in Touch

There is a famous quote that you network is your net worth. I knew of it but until I started living it, I didn't realise how true it was. As I got out there and met people on a consistent basis and made the effort to stay in touch via email or social media, I noticed that when I released something new it was so much easier to sell it to those that already knew, liked and trusted me. Social media is one way to keep in touch with those you meet but ultimately you don't own your contacts via social media. You are at the mercy of who gets to see what and certainly not all your connections see what you post.

Email and building a database of contacts that you meet or those that subscribe to get something from you is the best way to nurture contacts, stay in touch and make offers. There is another famous saying 'the money is in the list' which is also 100% true. I have seen people buy from me immediately, after months three, five and even nine years of being on my list. My job is not to wait but to focus on adding value and sharing my expertise that my list finds helpful. That and being connected on social media with those I actually meet where I add more value is the key to long-term success.

When deciding to build a database of your contacts, you will need to use a special platform called a CRM (Customer Relationship Manager). These platforms store your contacts, enable you to do mass email outs and you have the ability to segment your list as well as automate emails from it. There are many options on the market. For start-ups most begin with Mailchimp which is free to use, with paid options down the track. More established businesses go to Ontraport, Infusionsoft or Active Campaign. These have monthly subscription fees and greater functionality.

If you don't know how to set up your platform, there are people you can hire via Upwork that can help you out and maybe even provide you with some training on how to operate and manage it yourself. From there on in, your goal is to build your list. Always seek permission with those you meet if you want to add them to your list to stay in touch. Online when people opt in to get something from you then they are electronically giving you permission by inputting their name and email.

The other questions I get a lot is: how often should I email my database? There really isn't a right answer I can give you here. I am on lists where they email out three times a day and others once a month. I personally do it twice a week on a Tuesday and Thursday. I specifically choose to do it on those days for a higher likelihood that my emails will be read. On Monday people's inboxes are way too full and Friday they are finishing up for the week so I avoid those days. You need to decide for yourself what feels right for you and what you can commit to on a weekly basis. The key here is to build the consistency muscle. My recommendation is to start once a week and build it up to two or three times.

Writing the emails
The best emails are those that you feel the company or person from the other end is just speaking to you. They are not even too glitzed up with images or graphic design. They simply look like an email from a friend. You don't need to worry about all that pretty

stuff. The most important thing is to share valuable information and content with your database that makes them stick around – and in time, contact you or buy your book.

A one-page email is long enough as people are time poor. Make sure that it is well paragraphed so it can also be easily scanned. Use bullet points wherever possible and don't make your paragraphs too chunky. Lastly choose your subject line wisely. These need to be curiosity driven and interesting for people to click through and open your emails to find out more. Avoid having a subject line that is clickbait to increase your open rates. It will not make people happy and they will unsubscribe.

I recommend setting a particular time each week that you will write your emails so that it always happens. I do it on Mondays after I have done my weekly live streams and generally my content is from what I have just spoken about. Your email can then be also expanded upon to build your blog piece.

Remember, not everyone is ready to buy today. Keeping in touch is key to any business and author success. Top of mind is where you want to be within other people's heads. Ask any famous author if they have a database and I can guarantee you, the answer will be yes.

Strategy 35: Your Super Signature

At the end of every email there is a signature. This signature is super valuable real estate when it comes to your call to action or making people aware you have other things they can check out. I am going to share two different signatures I use for my emails. The first one is for emails that I send out on a daily basis between my clients or those that directly email me. It's not the ones I send out from the database. This signature looks visually much nicer and more personal. Here it is:

HI-TECH SUCCESS (ONLINE EXPOSURE & POWER)

Warm regards,

M: +61 412 085 160
E: natasa@natasadenman.com
W: www.natasadenman.com

GET BOOKS AND PLANNERS HERE

All the images and icons are clickable and take you where you can buy the books and planners. It has my personal branding logo, my photo and social media connect icons. You can hire someone on Fiverr or Upwork to create something like this for you very inexpensively.

My second signature is the one I use in my database emails. This one gives my readers a few different things they can do if they are ready to take the next steps. I actually saw this in a few other entrepreneurs emails and then read about it in a book which made me decide to create one for myself.

To Your Authoring Success,

Natasa Denman

Ultimate 48 Hour Author CEO/Founder

P.S. Whenever you're ready... here are 4 ways I can help you write or publish your book

1. Download Your Free Book of 'Shut-Up and Write your First Book' Find out the 48 Reasons that Stand in Your Way (click here)

2. Join Free the Ultimate 48 Hour Author Academy

Get immediate access to the latest training and online courses that will fast-track your writing and have you excited about the possibilities (click here)

3. Want to learn how to Write, Publish and Leverage Your First Book?

Book your place at our next Signature Blueprint for Ultimate Book Writing Success Online Seminar – The Best Non-Fiction Writing Seminar on the market.

AUSTRALIA/NZ Seminars (click here)

USA/Canada Seminars (click here)

If you have been to one in the past and want to book a Qualifying Chat for a Retreat click here

4. Ready to Publish?

Book a chat with our experienced team to find out what option is best for you (click here)

This signature has all the various ways people can get further involved with us and clickable areas to get to the next step. This enables me to leave my emails purely with valuable content without being promotional. It simply gives my readers the options for when they are ready and what they can do. If people have enjoyed getting my emails and staying in touch, one day they will click through and do something else if they are serious about writing their book.

You may not have as much as I do in my Super Signature. Start with one thing and build from there. You can simply say that they can download a sample of your book as one of your options.

Strategy 36: Ebook & Audio Book

If you want to make the most out of your book and generate more sales, you need to start thinking about the different ways people like to learn and consume content. Some like to hold on to a book to read, others read off their mobile devices and some like to listen to audiobooks as they go from place to place.

Aside from having your book available only as a paperback copy, it is really important to also convert it into an ebook and audiobook format. I always recommend to my authors to plan and stagger their launch dates for each format of their books, so that they can get the biggest impact and exposure each time they launch. The ideal gap between launches is 3–6 months. First you launch the paperback, then the ebook and lastly the audiobook.

Ebooks are great to use for lead generation if you choose to offer your book for free to generate more enquiries, especially if you are writing your book for business purposes. Or at the very least you can do the same with extracting just a sample of your book to be viewed as an ebook. Amazon does this amazingly well with books they have for sale. An ebook version of your book should be able to be converted from the paperback copy and your layout designer should be able to complete this for you easily.

When it comes to an audiobook, there are some considerations and planning to make it happen. The first thing you need to decide is whether you will speak out the content or get a narrator for it. If you have a great voice and want to make it super personal, then you are the one that should speak it out. If you have a heavy accent and are not sure if you will do a good job of the recording, then consider having a narrator. When having a narrator, you literally hand it over to the person helping you with the creation of your audiobook and wait for the final result.

In our company we have a contact that completes all the steps, including finding the female or male narrator, getting them to do the recording, cleaning up the audios, pulling it all together and then completing the distribution. The main audiobook resellers include:

Audible, Amazon, iTunes, Nook, Barnes & Noble, Audiobooks.com, Scribd., Reado.com, Audiobooksnow, Talking Bookz, Audiomol, Downpour, Playter, Follett, Audiobookstore.com, Bookmate, Findaway, Baker & Taylor, Hummingbird, Perma-Bound, Google Play, Hoopla, Rakuten Kobo, Libro.fm, Mofibo, 3Leaf Group, OverDrive, Mackin, eStories, Odilo, Bibliotheca + 3M, Storytel, Audioteka and ESBCO.

If you plan on recording your own audiobook, the process can be a little cheaper, but you still may need help with some of the other steps. Our audio contact advises our authors where to go to record their book as the type of studio and recording equipment is super important. Then the author sends in their recordings for the clean-up and other steps that come afterwards.

Audiobooks and ebooks are generally priced lower than paperback books as there are no costs in delivering them to a reader. All that happens instantly as soon as the reader makes a payment for the ebook or audiobook. It is worth the effort getting all this done so that you can further multiply your selling efforts of your book.

SECTION 5

SCALE UP
(TIME FOR LEVERAGE)

If you are serious about greater impact and transformation for your readers, you must start to think bigger. How can you further contribute to their lives and in turn be rewarded for this?

The following strategies will enable you to get creative, think further than your book and build greater infrastructure within which the book is the central point that everything else comes from. These are not for the light hearted – they require commitment, discipline and in some cases investment of your own money to make more money. Proceed with caution, but also know that for the courageous the rewards are often the greatest.

SCALE UP (TIME FOR LEVERAGE)

Strategy 37: Amazon #1 Best Seller

Becoming an Amazon #1 Best Seller has become one of the highly coveted goals that today's authors look to achieve. The credibility it adds to a book helps that author promote their title and win business much easier due to the perception this round golden sticker carries. It can be added to introductions and author bios and plastered all over websites and marketing collateral. My authors consistently ask for help in getting their books to be #1 Amazon Best Sellers.

One thing to note is that this is a strategy and a hack that clever authors execute for greater credibility. I will break it down in a short summary for you here. It is a process that requires techie knowledge and timing in order to be executed correctly and successfully. This strategy does not mean you are going to get rich by selling books, it is simply a boost for your and your book's profile.

The key is to understand first of all how Amazon works. They are just like Google, a search engine that works on keywords and categories and it has algorithms that update every few hours. Some keywords are highly searched, and some are not. Also, some categories are highly competitive, and some are not. There are tools you can use to do your research and discover what is relevant to your book but not as competitive.

Once you know this, you can start thinking about when you would like to launch your ebook on Amazon. Usually, the best days are a Tuesday, Wednesday and Thursday. These days people will most likely take action and buy your book. Ahead of your launch day you may also ask a group of close family and friends be part of your launch team, whereby they will buy your ebook and leave you a review. This is not always necessary, but every little bit helps.

A few days before launch day, you will upload your ebook and place it in the categories and keywords you researched to work best and be the least competitive. With your seven most searched keywords you also need to create a 500-word keyword rich description for your book. This is not just the blurb from the back of your book, but something that elaborates more about what readers are going to get from reading it. Here is an example from one of our authors that we researched and wrote for her. In bold are her highly searched relevant keywords.

500-word keyword rich description

Are you a woman over the age of 50 who is feeling a bit lost? Have you fallen out of love with your body and wardrobe? Do you wish above all else you could feel confident and alive again? You are not alone, as this is what a lot of women experience as they move into their 50s and beyond.

There is so much more than just knowing **how to dress** and **shopping for clothes.**

This must-read book by professional stylist and life-coach Moana Robinson, has been designed to empower you to take charge of this next stage of your life and rediscover your Sass and Style.

Moana is the founder of **B Styled for Life** and lives on the gorgeous Gold Coast on Australia's East Coast where she uses her personal styling, life-coaching and hypnotherapy to work with her clients on a wide range of their disempowering beliefs, with an area of focus on **women in business styles** to present themselves and their brand in the best possible light.

It is empowering, educational and most of all, it is written for you, so that you can not only look your best, but feel good on the inside too. It is so much more than a **fashion tips book.**

By now you have lived through many of life's challenges and rewards. You have experienced highs and lows and have had many wonderful, and some not so wonderful experiences. You have loved and lost and maybe loved again. You may be wondering what is ahead and whether you are making the most of your life. You don't want your lack of confidence to hold you back and are looking for more than just **fashion tips**, or a **personal style book**.

And this is the exciting part! With just a few tweaks and small changes in your beliefs – and your wardrobe – the most exciting part of your life journey is yet to come and your **Style Self-Esteem** will go through the roof!

Imagine, what your life would look like if you could live it free from doubt and you were filled with self-confidence. What would you try? What you say YES to more often?

Your own personal style develops, as does your **style confidence**, as you go through all the changes in life and even though you might not be a 25-year-old size 8, you can look and feel better than ever before.

Over 50s' fashion doesn't need to make you feel like your grandmother, but just as importantly, it doesn't need to make you look like a 16-year-old at the plaza.

The time has come now to recognise the opportunities that are before you and use these *'Wisdom Years'* to develop that SASS and STYLE that is uniquely yours and yours alone. This eye-opening book includes:

- Confidence and practical life tips in the first half of the book from Moana as a qualified life coach to help you understand your beliefs, fears and the shackles you have placed on yourself.
- Styling know how and practical information to sort your wardrobe and image to help you look your best for every occasion
- Top tips and tricks shared to make your life and style easier to manage for all budgets, body shapes and sizes
- Looks for **women in business**, casual lunches, nights out with friends and everywhere in-between.

The book will take up to 72 hours to go live on Amazon. The night before your launch day you will drop your ebook price down to 99 cents. This will remove any price objections in people's support of your ebook launch.

On the morning of your launch day, you will announce that you are launching your ebook on Amazon and for the next 24 hours only, it is offered at just 99 cents. Creating some nice images in Canva with your book cover and a simple link where people can get it helps a lot in getting traction. Writing some posts, an email to your database and sharing this announcement everywhere is key.

While you are launching and spreading the word far and wide, ensure that you monitor your ranking on Amazon. Watch how many downloads you are getting and where you are sitting with your ranking of your book.

Here is a sample of the previously mentioned author's launch day posts and the email we wrote for her database. Included are also some of her book promotion images we created for her.

Social media post 1

It is with great excitement that my book, *B Styled for Life – Living with Sass and Style Over 50* is launching on Amazon today!

When my book was published in late 2019, I was blown away by the feedback by those that read it and with orders in countries all around the world, I knew I needed to get it on the biggest online platform possible.

The best news about launching on Amazon is that for the next 24 hours, I am able to offer it for the launch price of just 99 cents.

B Styled for Life is so much more than a personal styling book. It is a complete overhaul of your mind, body and soul to let you live your best life as you are heading into your 50s and beyond.

If you are ready to live with Sass and Style, get your copy here (insert link) for only 99 cents until midnight tonight.

Social media post 2

Launching internationally today! *B Styled for Life – Living with Sass and Style Over 50* is now on Amazon and available for the next 24 hours for just 99 cents.

Want to get a copy?

If you are, or know a woman over the age of 50 who is feeling a bit lost, or might have fallen out of love with your body and wardrobe and wish above all else you could feel confident and alive again, then get a copy for 99 cents here (insert link).

I want to change the way so many women feel about themselves and with *B Styled for Life* they will begin their journey to 'Living with Sass and Style'

Buy your copy today (insert link)

Email to the database

Today is a big day.

One that I know I will cherish in the years to come when I look back on it.

Today is the day that my book, **B Styled for Life – Living with Sass and Style Over 50** is officially launching internationally on Amazon!

I will fulfill a dream of helping as many women as I can, fall back in love with themselves by understanding how they can be kinder to themselves, love what they have got, and look and feel great all the time.

This book helps women over 50 realise their own unique Sass and Style and has already been purchased via my website in six countries but now that it is launching worldwide, its ripples can spread far and wide.

I want to make a big impact, who has got time for playing small am I right?

So, **B Styled for Life** will be available for the next 24 hours for **only 99 US cents**.

<insert link here>

We are strongest together, and as women, when we unite and hold each other up, there is nothing that we can't achieve and if my book can reach those that need it most, I will have achieved some level of contribution that is a huge key to fulfilment and happiness.

Join with me and celebrate all the amazing women, who sacrifice so much for so many who might just need a little bit back in return.

Purchase a copy for you, a friend or loved one for **only 99 US cents** <insert link here>

Living with Sass and Style,

Mo x

'Wow, reading the book now. Oh my god! ... they are all the words I say ... Just wonderful. Every woman over 50 should read this book. It is a must read!' – **Julie Tengdahl, Award Winning Australian Fashion Designer/Artisan**

'I love the way this book is written! Moana has used her many years in styling, coaching and life lessons to deliver a practical book filled with styling know-how, action steps and activities designed to live with sass and style when you're over 50! Interested in a style guide with a difference then this is the book for you!' – **Toni Lontis, Author, TV and Radio Host**

'Sometimes you come across a book and you know it was written for you. Well Moana's book is one of them. **B Styled for Life – Living with Sass and Style over 50** has so many great points in it, that I think I highlighted nearly every page! She talks about the real-life challenges we face as middle aged women, tips to navigate them and also ways to truly live a sassy life – **Shar Moore, Author, Publisher and Keynote Speaker**

Launch day
With all this at the ready, launch day also needs to have a plan. Here is the sample plan of what we do or tell our authors to do:

Plan Sheet for Your Amazon Best Seller Launch Day

Dear Author,

Please take action on the outlined tasks on your launch day using the copy and promotional images that we have or will be supplying to you closer to your launch day.

Send the pre-written email out at 8am to your full database.
Put one post on your Facebook Personal Profile at 8am (make sure your image is attached as well as the tinyurl listed in the post).

Live Stream at 8:30am for 5–20 mins talking about your book, tips and encouraging listeners to get it today only for 99 cents.

8am post on LinkedIn.
8am post on Instagram or all other social media platforms you are a member of.
8:30am post on any Facebook Groups you are a member of and where it is allowed.

9am get people with big networks to post about your book launch. You may need to ask ahead of time and give these people an image and a suggested post so you make their life easy. Not everyone will be able to do this, but certainly have a think and try to find people that have large networks that can support you.

10am post on your Business/Fan/Like Page
10am private message any contacts that have said will support you and continue to always reply to comments so that the post remains top of the news feed.

Midday – put up an article style post on LinkedIn

1pm update on personal FB profile, Instagram and LinkedIn about achieving #1 status and going for #1 on paid version. (Normally most authors we have helped hit #1 by 1pm on launch day)

5pm email your list making an announcement of #1 best seller and in which categories. Thank everyone for their support.

Make sure that throughout the whole day you are replying to comments and thanking people when they say they have bought it. The more you reply the more your posts stay at the top of the news feed.

Extra Boost Idea: Think about a Share & Win option! Could you offer a valuable prize, gift voucher or other gift that will have a wide appeal. The idea is that this will encourage your friends to share your post from your personal profile. Make sure your post is public otherwise it cannot be shared.

Here is an example from one of my #1 Campaign days. (Image created on Canva)

Post copy:

In light of my latest book launching today, amongst the celebrations, I've decided to offer a fun little giveaway to 3 people that take part in the fun. The rules are simple:

1. Share this post if you think your network would love to get their hands on the hot deal today only.
2. Comment on this post that your share has been done and choose the additional book from the list below you'd love to have.
3. I'll enter you in the draw to win. Three names will be draw on my live stream at 9pm Melbourne time tonight.

If you WIN, I will post you:

Paperback copy of Fully Booked Retreats
PLUS a choice of a paperback copy from one of these:
- Ultimate 48 Hour Author
- Shut up and Write Your First Book
- Bums on Seats
- 1000 Days to Million Dollar Coaching Business from Home
- Ninja Couch Marketing
- The 7 Ultimate Secrets to Weight Loss

Good luck!!!

Monitoring your ranking

Make sure you are available and glued to your computer during the entirety of your launch day. You need to be posting, responding, following up and announcing when you hit #1 Best Seller. Here is an image of where your ranking on Amazon is and what it will look like when you hit #1.

Product details
Format: Kindle Edition
File Size: 3044 KB
Print Length: 166 pages
Simultaneous Device Usage: Unlimited
Publisher: Ultimate World Publishing (25 February 2020)
Sold by: Amazon Australia Services, Inc.
Language: English
ASIN: B0856S7M9V
Text-to-Speech: Enabled
X-Ray: Not Enabled
Word Wise: Enabled
Screen Reader: Supported
Enhanced Typesetting: Enabled
Customer Reviews: ☆☆☆☆☆ 1 customer review
Amazon Bestsellers Rank: #57 Paid in Kindle Store (See Top 100 Paid in Kindle Store)
   #1 in Style & Clothing
   #1 in Beauty & Fashion (Kindle Store)
   #8 in Self-Help (Books)

When you see this, start taking your screenshots as proof that you are #1 Best Seller and in the various categories. You may hit #1 in 2–3 categories which is awesome. When this happens, it is time to announce it everywhere and put the stamp on your book. Here it is the way it looks after a book is number #1.

The stamp is placed by your cover designer and for any printed books without stamps you can get stickers. I got stickers designed and made for my authors that I post out to them. Amazon does not give you this stuff – you need to create it yourself and reupload the new cover there and update it for your next physical copies print run.

So, there you go!!! A brief description of how this process unfolds. How will you know if this gets more of your books sold? Who knows? It's one of those intangible statuses that improve a book's credibility and an author's profile, but it is a hard thing to measure true return on investment.

Should you attempt it on your own? You can if you know what you are doing and are tech savvy. Most of our authors choose against it as they don't want to spend the time learning how to do it while they can be focusing on their own expertise, so they ask us to help.

Strategy 38: Your Book's Fan/Business Page

Yes, we are about to start talking social media!!! It's one of those things in today's world that you must master if you want to be a successful author. In the next five strategies I am going to break down for you the different parts of social media for your book, as I believe they are all important to do and have set up correctly. So, let's begin with your book's Fan Page. This is also sometimes called a business page or like page on Facebook. We will focus on Facebook as it is the most widely used platform with varying functionality. Those that avoid social media or just tap in and out of it randomly are robbing themselves of success and abundance in so many ways. It's a necessary evil as they say and creating a strategy and plan with it, should help you avoid the time wasting that can occur while on social.

As your book is your business, or you may have a business behind your book, it needs to have its own business page on Facebook. After all you are not meant to be promotional on your personal profile. It is only through your business page that you can run promotions and ultimately ads. When you think about your Fan Page, think of it as your website on social media. You must have it as people will stalk you to check out more of what you do. It needs to contain valuable posts, images, videos and stay active and current so that you remain credible and look like you are around.

Once you have worked on your strategy and plan for your Fan Page, you can outsource the management of it and posting to a virtual assistant. You can curate content and they can post and respond, or you can have them curate the content around your message and you just approve it to go live so you save even more time.

Your Fan Page has many functions and areas people can explore such as Shop, Services, Offers, Events, Community, etc. It is important to have all the correct information set up on there and to keep adding to it and going through it every six months to ensure what you have there is current and updated. It truly operates like a website in so many ways. Checking out people on social media is way more common nowadays over reading their usually very static websites.

Ensure that you use a great profile photo for your Fan Page, and in your cover photo have your book in the image. Set up your Shop area so browsers can click on and buy your book from there.

Important note on Fan Pages: As Facebook wants businesses to spend money on advertising, they don't show the posts that you put up on your fan page to many people. Your reach will be very low for organically posted posts. So, should you boost them? I don't recommend that you do unless it is for a specific purpose. We will talk about paid advertising in a later strategy. Don't be disheartened if you don't see many people liking or commenting on your posts. The most important thing is that you are consistently posting and having current posts on there. The purpose of this is because when people go to stalk your profile and click on your Fan Page, you want them to see that you are active, involved and committed to your book and business success.

Speaking of business, if you already have a Fan Page for your business, you do not need to start another one. Just ensure that your book cover appears in your cover photo and you set it up in the Shop area available for purchase. No need to double up. If you don't have a business behind your book, then name your Fan Page your book title or something related to the niche you are writing for. Connect your Fan Page to your website by listing your website in the description, and vice versa on your website have an icon that can take visitors to your Fan Page. It's the best way to grow your likes and audience.

Strategy 39: Demystifying Facebook Groups

When thinking about Facebook groups, I'd like you to think communities of the virtual variety. They are groups of people with like interests that have come together for a specific purpose. There are many different types of groups and perhaps you are a member of some. Via the Fan Page we were discussing earlier, the conversation tends to be one sided with only the Fan Page posts on its wall and then replies to any comments on those posts. Within Facebook groups all members can post on the group's wall and other members get involved in the discussion, so it is a two-way conversation with much more variety. So, how does your book fit into the world of Facebook groups?

Before starting your own group, it's a great idea to be an active member of other people's groups that may contain similar conversations that you are planning to lead when you start your own. You can check out what you like, what you don't like and get ideas on how to engage the group and what to post. Like with anything in life, we first watch other people do something, then we learn it for ourselves and finally take action on it. It is really important to read other group's rules to be familiar with what you can and can't do. Think about how you can add value rather than rock up and be self-promotional. It's virtual networking after all and relationships need to be developed before you ever consider posting a special promotion.

So many people get this wrong and they think if they can post in 100 groups about their awesome book, some book sales are going to eventuate. What you are likely to do, is piss off a lot of group owners and get banned from a lot of groups for self-promotion. Don't do that!!! Think about interesting things you can share, questions you can ask and comments and advice you can impart with other group members. The more people see you active in a group, the more familiar you become and if people like what you have to say, they will naturally look you up and check out what you are about. You don't even need to tell them what you do and what you have to sell.

When it comes time to start your own group, you need to think about the name and type of group. There are three types of groups: Open that anyone can join, Closed that people can apply to join and be approved and Secret where only you the owner or an admin can add members into it. I own Closed and Secret groups on my Facebook. One is called Ultimate Business Support which is a wider niche for small business owners, and one is called Author Your Way to Riches which is niched for those budding authors. My secret group is called Ultimate 48 Hour Author Mastermind and it is only for my paying clients and inner circle community that I have helped write books.

The purpose of each group is different. In the business one, I share small business tips and always suggest that writing a book is great for business. Through this I open up awareness to those business owners that have never considered writing a book for their business. In the Author Your Way to Riches one, I share tips for first-time authors on how they can succeed with their book (writing and promoting it). Here I hope that some of the group will reach out and ask our business to help them achieve this dream. In my secret group, I want to make my own clients feel super special and connected only with those that are on the same journey as themselves. We all speak the same language, use the same system and understand what happens in-house. I also like to think about groups as a social media sales funnel where you tend to have the most members in the broader niched ones and least in the ones you are working with that have committed to get help from you.

When you create your own group, you are responsible to monitor, manage, drive engagement and encourage participation. You set the rules and therefore you are the one that is likely to reap the greatest rewards for all your efforts. You are stepping into a leadership position that many try to avoid. When naming your group, don't name it the name of your book. Instead think about the niche and the issue behind your book that people would want to discuss. This way your group will be a lot easier to find and resonate with your ideal future members. Book sales happen because you become a person of influence that is leading a community and sharing freely. People buy people!!! Being a first-time author you must get others to get to know you first before they are ready to buy from you.

Strategy 40: Your Personal Profile

The highest reach you will get on your posts will be on your personal profile. Many of my authors have big resistance to using their personal profiles. I don't understand why, as I know how passionate they are about their message. I say that you never have to share things you are not comfortable in sharing on your personal profile, but you do need to be active and get your friends supporting what you do. When people see others supporting you and commenting, it drives more interaction and comments from those that may not comment or interact usually. Many others are also just watching and observing without you knowing. If you also make your personal profile public, your posts can be seen by those that are not even your friends.

We find our authors always get the greatest traction with their pre-launch campaign when they post on their personal profile. After all, this is where your warm audience hangs out, those that like, know and trust you. They will be your first followers on this first-time author journey. Allow them in and behind the scenes of what you are doing. Here is a template post we encourage our authors to put up on the first day of their retreat on their personal profile. They can adjust it anyway they like and alongside it they put the mock-up cover of their book as well as a payment link to start taking pre-sales.

Social media post for day 1

I am so excited – as some of you may know, and many others may not, I have decided it is time to step up and write my first book.

I am currently at The Ultimate 48 Hour Author Retreat in Victoria and by this time on Sunday I will have completed my book.

SCALE UP (TIME FOR LEVERAGE)

Just a few minutes ago the facilitators running this event issued us all a challenge. And I need your help to win.

We are seeing who can sell the most books by the end of the three days, which is so exciting and a bit scary at the same time.

My book is called <insert name here> and I am writing it because <insert reason/who it will help/why it needs to be written> to help <target reader>.

My book will be back from the publishers in <insert desired timeline here> and will sell for $29.95 <or insert your sell price here> yet I have decided to offer it for sale at a pre-release price of $19.95 plus $5 postage Australia wide.

Either comment below if you are interested in being one of the first to get a copy of <insert name again here> or would like to support me on my journey to published author.

Watch this space.

Woohoo!

Those that have been active on social media in the past we see easily sell more than 50 books over the first 48 hours. Others that have not been active, still sell a handful at the very least. The record stands at 444 in the first 48 hours by one author at a past retreat. The best thing about this strategy is how much excitement it brings to the authors as they are writing their books and how it backs their commitment to completion.

Your personal profile is powerful, and you do not need to be self-promotional to make it work. Yes, the post above is, however it is written in such a way that it's more of an exciting announcement over an ad. With your personal profile you can take your friends and followers on a journey as you are writing your book, updating them of what stage you are at and sharing valuable tips and stories from within your book by doing lives and posting some quotes and images. This is where your readers/clients can also get to know you on a more personal level of what you like to do and who you hang out with. I freely share all about my travels, family, things I see, do and experience. When I run into people in real life, often they tell me about things I have done and ask me questions about my life that I don't realise I have posted about. It kind of helps not having to repeat yourself every single time you see someone. I am the same with others and this keeps our connection much stronger even though we are not together all the time. I feel I have such close contacts all over Australia, USA and Canada because I have connected and stay connected with these people online regularly.

Make sure your personal profile is also well filled out and set up. Your personal details, your Fan Page, website and anything that you want people to know when they arrive at your profile matters. Avoid using cat and dog profile images. Put you best face forward every single time. You also have a cover photo on your profile that you can have updated regularly, and you can have yourself there holding your book. I actually hold one of my books in my personal profile photo. So, don't be shy, get known and get personal!!!

Strategy 41: What the Heck Do I Post?

Being successful on social media and generating lots of engagement has a lot to do with what you post. People use social media mostly for entertainment purposes and connecting, so it is key to think about that before you post. The key word I want you to remember is VARIETY! Here I would like to share with you some ideas of the variety I am talking about. By mixing up these ideas you can build out a social media post calendar and eventually outsource this for someone else to take over for you. Here is a list of ideas for the types of post you can put up:

- Plain text posts (least recommended as they don't catch the eye). If you are going to do something that is plain text, keep it short and put in one of those colourful backgrounds that Facebook has ready to go. This will make it stand out. I suggest putting quotes or questions like this.
- Image with text post – lengthier written posts do not fit in those backgrounds and yes you can still put them on but attach a photo that makes sense with the text that you are writing.
- Short videos where you share a tip or a story that have been pre-recorded.
- Live stream once a week for longer than 10 minutes and share your thinking, message and engage with a live audience.
- Share something that is helping you in your life like a tool, app, appliance, etc. It doesn't have to be book or business related just simply be helpful to others on a human level.
- Funny memes that you may have found on the internet or you create yourself. These are very shareable and can give you great exposure far and wide.
- Use Canva to create beautifully designed images with text over the top of them. I mentioned this earlier in the book when I showed you my branded quotes. Refer back to that for ideas.
- Think about the time of the year that it is and how that relates to something you may write about. The other day it was Valentine's day and my content got linked up to love in a roundabout way so that it is relevant in terms

of what most people are thinking about. I often come up with my content as I think about what is going on and how I feel or what is happening to me at that time.
- Questions, questions, questions – they really drive the most engagement. Use this one at least once a week.

Hopefully that list will help you build out what each week may look like for you. You can rotate through the variety of posts time and time again. No-one will notice what you are doing, but they will stay engaged with what you post. Some people choose to write their social posts ahead of time and others set aside some time each day. I have done both and don't really have a preference. I just make sure I do it!!!

Every social media platform is also slightly different. The above ideas work best for Facebook, but when you think about LinkedIn, Instagram, Tik Tok, Pinterest, YouTube, then you need to observe the culture within these platforms. Some are more professional, some are image heavy, video only and so on. Facebook is kind of a mixed bag of them all and if you get that one right, you are likely to also thrive on the others. You will just need to follow the format that most use on each of the other platforms.

Remember, social media is meant to be fun and enjoyable for people. It is where we really connect. That is what wins business. It's no longer an advertise and sell type of economy. In today's world we live in an education-based value of information economy. People need to see value, get to know us, build familiarity and then they buy. This takes time to build but when it does, you have built a base of raving fans that will snap up anything you put in front of them.

Strategy 42: To Pay for Ads or Not to Pay for Ads?

Tapping into the world of paid advertising isn't for the light-hearted. The initial stages of testing and measuring can seem like you are haemorrhaging a lot of money and seeing no results. I definitely do not recommend simply running ads for people to buy your book. It just doesn't work.

With paid advertising you really need to think about the big picture and how it all connects. Those of you that have your book as a way to leverage your business are ideal candidates for paid ads and may have even done this in the past. I don't recommend this strategy for memoirs only. Here are some suggestions of how a book can be used in paid advertising to drive more leads and enquiries into your business:

1. Give it away totally FREE as an ebook – I did this with the first version of my Ultimate 48 Hour Author book and it was generating 65% conversion with those that clicked on my ad at the time. This grew my database significantly. That was the intention and eventually those that ended up on my database, came along and did my program after a period of value adding and nurturing. The one thing I did learn though, is that getting a full free book is great, however, it's too much information which means people are not likely to read it. So, I swapped this strategy to giving away a four-page PDF of the key summary points from my book with a call to action at the end of it. We called it the Magic PDF.

2. Send ads to a Free paperback book but charge postage only – you may have seen this one out there on social

media. The author offers their full paperback book for free and all they ask for is that you cover the postage of $9.95. Generally, this amount would cover both printing and shipping of the book. The intention of this author is once again to build their following and database and they have lined up a series of automated next steps of engaging with those that take action so that they end up buying more from them to solve their problem.

3. Send ads to videos or value-adding content to build an audience that you will re-target later – this once again is not going to initially be a money-making strategy as you are simply sending people to an information piece that they may find interesting. However, when they click on it, this indicates they have interest in that information so that when later on you are sending out ads with a call to action, people will be re-targeted and see you pop up again. This makes you familiar to them and therefore they are more likely to take the next step with you.

4. Send ads to a Free or low-cost event – this is really effective as it shows you as being generous with your information and willing to share solutions via events. It is at the event you can then upsell to books and other services if you are in business. Events truly are something to master if you want your message to spread far and wide. We have also found that depending on your credibility in the marketplace you are advertising and the culture of that country, one or the other may work better. When people sign up for your event, you can also think about setting a VIP option upgrade and for those that are really committed they will snap that up. Refer back to Strategy 10 to review this suggestion.

5. Send ads to a Free assessment or quiz – everyone loves to test themselves and have their result emailed to them. A great example I have noticed lately on Facebook ads are those intermittent fasting ads that drive you to answer some questions in order to determine which type of fasting is best suited to your body type, age and activity levels. In our business we did a quiz on people's readiness to write their first books. Once people take the quiz, the opportunity is there to offer them the next step in the solution. For the intermittent fasting ads, it would be either a customised menu you can purchase or meals you can have delivered. For us it was to invite our audience to take part in our half-day seminar.

6. Send ads to a Free or low-cost 30-day challenge – yet again this is a way to build your database and spend more time with people to build like, know and trust. With these challenges you have the opportunity at the end to upsell to the next step in your solution. They are a taste and offer huge value. Those that are fully committed will take those next steps. You can also offer smaller paid deals throughout as you seed towards the final one.

In a nutshell, ads are about drawing an audience to you. Getting them to enter your world and database and continuing the relationship. It's not about massive sales. It may work that way for some products out in the marketplace, but it doesn't work the same way for information-based products such as books. You must be more strategic and think of the long-term game you are playing.

Whatever you do, do not attempt posting ads on your own. Hire an expert that knows what they are doing and work alongside them. Listen to what they say, make suggestions and give them whatever content they request from you. Record videos they need and be an active participant in the relationship. They are responsible for knowing the ever-changing make-up of Facebook or whatever platform you plan to advertise on. They will monitor and make changes as they are testing and measuring along the way. Do not give up on someone too quickly. Minimum engagement should be three months to really get things moving. The more you advertise, the better results you will see as people will start to get that repetition on seeing your ads and one day click through to take part. I know this as we have been doing ads for seven years now and have been through all sorts of ups and downs on the journey, but it's been totally worth it as this is the reason the business expanded nationally and internationally.

Don't start too early either. Make sure you have a proven system that has sold before. Use the measure that you have made at least $10,000 in your niche before taking the plunge into ad world. When you do, always test and measure your results and revenue from it. You must know your numbers and conversion rates to then continue advertising with confidence.

Strategy 43: Plaster it Everywhere

First-time authors tend to be very shy when it comes to showing off their achievement in writing a book. Perhaps it's the fear of standing out, or of criticism, or simply the biggest one of all – success!!! They end up the biggest kept secret with a garage full of books. Let's not do that. Thus far, I have shared so many strategies that you can take action on to ensure that never happens. As much as I remind my authors to show off their book in all places they tend to forget. So, here I am going to give you a checklist of where it should appear:

- ✓ Website banner so that it follows people no matter what page they are on

SCALE UP (TIME FOR LEVERAGE)

- ✓ Website shop/book page so people can buy it
- ✓ Your email signature with you holding your book
- ✓ Your pull-up banner for any face-to-face promotions
- ✓ In your office behind you as a background so each time you are on calls it's there sending subconscious messages to people as they talk or listen to you
- ✓ The back of your business cards – don't waste valuable real estate on there
- ✓ Branded clothing like T-shirts you may make
- ✓ Flyers or brochures that promote your business and book
- ✓ Order forms
- ✓ Your social media cover photos
- ✓ Bookmarks, branded tablecloths for expos
- ✓ Some social media posts like quotes from your book.

These are the main ones and most common ones. Every time you do something, ask yourself these questions:

- How does my book come into this?
- Who is likely to lay their eyes on this and could they be my ideal reader/client?
- If I put my book here will it improve my credibility and this piece of marketing collateral?

Please take my advice and complete the checklist. Keep it in your awareness at all times – you wrote your book as a tool towards your credibility, success and expert status. Don't hide it from people. Plaster it everywhere!!! If you don't like your cover after a while, just change it to refresh the look and then relaunch the new look. That is all that needs to happen!!! I've changed the cover of *Ultimate 48 Hour Author* three times in seven years.

Strategy 44: Online Program Creation

Online programs have really taken the world by storm. They are a great way to learn in a self-paced environment in the comfort of your own home. I've taken part in lots, have my own and my authors have created theirs. They can be free, low-cost or high-end depending on how much content you decide to put into them. I suggest a variety of all three in time. My favourite platform to host online programs is Teachable. It's sleek, professional and automates absolutely everything. There is a monthly subscription fee for it, but it's totally worth it if you are going to make online programs part of your intellectual property and offers for your readers/clients.

You can cross promote your book in all your online programs and vice versa you should advertise the fact you have an online program at the back of your book. If you didn't do that the first time, it's not too late. You can always add an extra page in the back for your book and update your book files.

The easiest way to create an online program is to record video content on the information you share within your book. If you book is say 12 chapters, then create 12 videos where you talk through the steps and then have templates and resources people can download alongside your videos. Zoom is a great platform to record your videos yourself simply speaking on screen. The wonderful thing is that it has screen sharing capabilities which means if you need to show something on the internet or your desktop while you are teaching you can easily do it and flick back and forth from screen sharing to you speaking.

Feel free to have bullet points nearby so that you can keep track of what you are teaching and so that you remember to say all you need to say in that lesson. It's not a bad thing to refer to notes.

If you don't want to appear that you are looking at notes on your side, then put them on post it notes on your computer screen and then you will be looking in the same spot the whole time. There are all sorts of tips and tricks when it comes to completing this easily.

When filming, your lighting and background are super important. Use the tools mentioned in Strategy 27 and ensure you have a clean and/or branded background. Keep it all consistent so it flows nicely for the person taking part in the course.

Remember to mention further ways people can do additional learning with you. This means they might like to buy the book for all the notes on what you are teaching, take part in the next course that delves deeper into the content or even join a particular group where you offer support. It all depends on what you have and what action you want your student to take next.

Once you learn how to pull together an online program, you will be able to smash out the future ones with ease. It simply takes some planning and a day of action to get it all filmed and set up. The first time it may not be that way, but other times I guarantee it will.

Strategy 45: What is Your Next Step?

From the beginning, I have always said that the secret to really monetising your book is to think bigger. The book is only the beginning of what you can offer the world. There is so much value within you that you can expand on to delve even deeper in showing people how to solve the problem you help with. Start thinking about your sales funnel. If someone does this, what do I want them to do next? Don't think that this is manipulative, think that you are able to help them more.

Books are simply information and knowledge, but when you can provide some implementation then you arrive at transformation. This is worth its weight in gold as they say. Your clients will be grateful they committed fully to their transformation and will say to you: I am so glad I did this properly – you have changed my life. I hear this all the time. You are not serving people if you just whet their appetite, and then don't provide more support on their journey to success in whatever endeavour. And guess what – if they liked what you said but you do not offer that next step, they will find someone else who does.

An author's sales funnel may look something like this: Free PDF checklists, templates, short reports, free online course, etc., that leads to the next step to buy the book, come to a low-cost seminar, do a low-cost online course, etc,. that leads to full high-end online course, group coaching, longer seminar or a multi-day event, etc., that leads to one-to-one customised service, high-end masterminds or done for your services.

You may not have every single one of these in your funnel, but those are some ideas you can start thinking about. Keep it simple over having too much to offer. The key is to figure out the 3–4 steps that people may take with you as they go through your funnel. When the formula works, you simply repeat it over and over and over. This is when you have arrived at a model that can be scaled, and you can get other people involved to service different parts in your business.

In business, you always start with the end in mind. If I do this, what will happen next? Ad hoc actions lead to ad hoc results. Stepping out with purpose, creating with purpose and posting with purpose will always yield you better outcomes. Be generous by sharing free content, but don't forget to ask for the sale so you can have the opportunity to help people deeper with implementation.

SCALE UP (TIME FOR LEVERAGE)

Strategy 46: Fun Competitions

Who doesn't love a fun competition where they have a chance to win a prize! People are generally competitive and love to win, so why not consider running some competitions from time to time. This requires some creativity. When done well, you can get lots of shares and exposure of your competition which in turn points people back to you to check out what you do. If your book is part of the competition that is even better. Earlier in Strategy 37 when we spoke about the Share and Win competition when I was running my Amazon Best Seller campaign, that was an example of an interactive competition that got people sharing and also promoted the fact I have all these other books people can check out.

To get your creative juices flowing simply google 'contest ideas' and you will find so many articles written by others suggesting all sorts of ways to generate engagement and contests on social media. Running a competition, can lead to greater awareness of what you have on offer. I remember the first time I was running the first Ultimate 48 Hour Author retreat, I offered a scholarship for one budding author to win. There was a full application process and interviews of the top three applicants. Then one person won and took part in this highly coveted program.

A few of the other applicants who didn't win still ended up paying for the full program months later as they really wanted to get their books done with us. The scholarship provided the awareness of us and this brand-new way of completing and publishing a first book.

Avoid simply having your book as the thing people can win. Think about bundling and matching up other products and/or services that will make it greater value and more attractive to others, so they do share and encourage others to take part. Make sure that you let everyone know when the competition ends and that you will draw the winner live online so that they can join and see who wins. Keep a tab of all those taking the action to be part of the draw and then decide which way you like to draw the winner.

You can use names in a hat, one of my authors used a type of little bingo numbering container that would spin around and then she picked a number out, or there are also online tools. If you google 'random name picker', you can enter all the names on there and then shuffle them to generate a winner. Super easy and no physical tools required. You can simply go live online via Zoom and share your screen so they can see it happening then and there.

Make sure that you contact your winner promptly, tag them in the post where they have won and organise the delivery of their prize also quickly. You can ask your winner to take a photo receiving their prize and put it on social for further exposure and interaction related to the competition.

This strategy may become something you may like to do two to four times a year to generate more leads and awareness. You may like to try different competitions to see what really works well and gives you the greatest results. To make it even more sophisticated in how people register, you may build a special competition only landing page that will collect the entrant's contact details and may have an automated thank you and good luck page. Then those people become part of your database and you have the opportunity to have regular communication with them until such time that they may unsubscribe or buy from you.

Strategy 47: Join a Community of Authors

Every author has their own journey with their books. As much as I teach all my authors to do the suggested strategies in this book, I still have a lot of them trying different things as they get ideas themselves. This is wonderful! Because when they do stumble upon a great strategy that works, they freely share what they did in our community of authors. All of a sudden, the value is greater and we all get to find out a different way to promote our books. I know that I don't have all the answers and that I have not tried everything when it comes to book sales and marketing. I have tried and actioned a hell of a lot but there still are unexplored ways to get attention for my books.

That is why I strongly encourage you to be part of a community of authors where you can follow their posts, what they did, how they did it and see what resonates with you when it comes to trying it with your book. We have two communities on Facebook. One is free to join and is called Author Your Way to Riches and the other is my Ultimate 48 Hour Author Mastermind which is our secret authors only group available to those that invested fully in our system and are doing things with their books actively. This is where the absolute gold is shared. Not only do they learn from one another and me weekly, they also end up collaborating on other projects outside of their books if there is a business connection/collaboration link.

What I have done in this book is asked a few of them to share with you some of their ideas of how they have marketed and sold their books. After the last strategy, you will find their write up on some of the unique things that have worked for them.

Communities of like-minded individuals with similar goals will really help and encourage you on your journey. It is always great to go into places where you are not the smartest person in the room in order to learn and be stretched by ideas you have never even considered. Your success will never end up being a solo effort. When you look back you will be able to connect the dots of the key people and colleagues that helped you on the way.

There are many online communities for authors. I suggest join a few to really get the feel for which one feels right for you. They will all have their own flavour. Some may only talk fiction, some memoirs or children's books, and others business leverage. Your community should reflect the type of goals you have with your book and an alignment with the genre you are writing in. When you find your tribe, you will certainly know.

Strategy 48: Read, Read, Read – Action, Action, Action

Welcome to the final strategy!!! You made it. Hopefully by now your head is full of ideas that you will unpack for yourself and start actioning to drive more books sales and business your way. However, our learning never stops. I continue to learn, read and listen from those ahead of me all the time. I am aware there is so much more to explore and try when it comes to authoring success. That is why we finish off on the fact that this should not be the first and only book that you read on this topic.

Other successful authors have also written books on book sales and marketing that may contain various new strategies you have not yet considered. Check them out. You will most likely find similarities in a lot of what we talk about, but also look for unique suggestions that were not in this book. I love searching for the gold nugget in a book that can change how I do things in my life/

business. I continue reading books on how to write a book, even though I have now written 13 of them. I do this so I can deepen my knowledge and expertise on the subject matter I am an expert in. So that I can make my authors' lives easier and smoother when it comes to working with me.

I remember when I read a suggestion in a book that when proofing your book you should read it out loud so that you slow down and this way you will be able to catch more errors or typos. This was a game changer for everyone. I had just never considered it myself. Ever since I started making that suggestion to my authors and took it on board myself, the quality of the books went from great to outstanding. Had I not read that in someone else's book as a suggestion, I may not have thought about this awesome and powerful tip.

Therefore, I don't only encourage you to read more books on sales and marketing for your book, but also on your key area of expertise. If you are a weight loss/health expert, keep on top of the information and books that share ideas on that. Read more books, listen to other people's ideas. You don't need to copy anyone, but use some of the insightful information as parts of what you recommend in your own style. After all, we are all a culmination of the information we have learnt from our teachers, parents, many books, seminars, mentors, videos, etc. As we have our own experiences, challenges and wins, we also interpret the information in a way that makes sense to us. This is why when we teach it, its unique and in our voice, with our stories and flavour. Embrace this, as it is your unique DNA of intellectual property.

Use the consumption of more material, as a way to unblock you as well. Sometimes I feel that I have run out of ideas for content and feel uninspired. The best thing I can do is to start reading some more, watch something inspiring or listen to a podcast. A trigger may be something I read, heard or watched and that one aha moment gets me going again with my own writing.

Lastly, as you learn and read more please don't forget to take action. I know many people who are lifelong learners and absolutely love it. This is great, but without implementation you will never have the life/business transformation that you are looking for. There are many that have spent more on their education than they will ever earn from what they have learnt. Don't add to the percentage of this group. Be in the top 3% that skyrocket their life and business and design their future by choice. Go out there and smash it out!!!

PART 2

Strategies from Real-Life Authors Getting Real-Life Results

SECTION 6

REAL-LIFE AUTHORS GETTING REAL-LIFE RESULTS

Anni Finsterer – Author of *Radical Rock and Roll Resilience*

Where there are people, there are opportunities
Natasa said something to me and I have burnt this into my own psyche. It is now my mantra.

'Wherever there are people, there are opportunities.' I took this saying and I ran with it.

(If you're ever feeling shy, this saying is a one fell swoop killer.)

When I got my book in hand, I decided I was going to get the book into shop windows.

Of course, as a self-published book, this can be tricky. My modus operandi was to bring joy and likes on my socials to the shop. I rang ahead to check if they were open to taking the book or I dropped one in for the consignment manager. (Consignment means they keep it on trial and return it to you if it doesn't sell.)

I followed up and when they agreed to take the book, I took five books in. I didn't ask about this. I just did it.

Then I asked if they'd mind featuring the book in the window so I could have a photo for socials and therefore promote their shop. They were always very happy to do this, especially as I was falling over myself with delight in an attempt for them to keep the book right where it was – in the window.

I tripled my social following by posting and tagged communities I am aligned with, incrementally overcoming my social media fears of judgement and shyness by posting about my book.

I updated my LinkedIn profile. I'm not sure how the Field Marketing Manager for Sitecore (your digital experiences at Bunnings and Jetstar are powered by Sitecore) found me and asked me to do a keynote for a major virtual event of the year, aimed at Sitecore customers, prospects and partners for 250–300 attendees. I took a leap of faith and with my best abundant mindset, asked for a hefty fee ($4000). She agreed to it. I am now waiting for confirmation on the run of events.

I have now reached out to two book distributors, so they can do the running around, and am waiting for a response.

When coronavirus hit in 2020, I waited for numbers to be increased to 30 people allowed in a public space and then pounced to organise a book launch party at a bar which will double as a singing gig for my band Anni and the Electric Fins.

I have booked a meeting with the actors centre to speak to young actors, (which I once was) and to have another launch there for a different crowd/older people.

I have booked two school speaking gigs for year 12 students (one in Sydney and one Canberra) for a young adult book club, as well as booking a webinar with a communications company. Now to organise a talk for different times and formats. This is the trickiest part!

Julie Fisher – Author of *The Unexpected Journey*

Care package success

Writing my book, *The Unexpected Journey*, was a dream that was realised after meeting Natasa and Stuart Denman. It was something I had always wanted to do and with the guidance and support given by them, my dream turned into a reality.

Once I was writing my book, and attending seminars with Natasa, a burning passion to create more started brewing. She taught me skills that I only thought would work in business, but after following her program, and learning to believe in myself, I have worked very hard and am now working with families to help them with support and advocacy for their children.

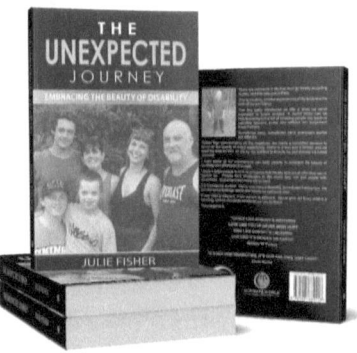

I have also started becoming active with many other Down Syndrome groups and through networking and reaching out to them, I have been able to collaborate with the group Celebrate T21. They provide care packages to new families of children with Down Syndrome which includes many lovely products for the children, as well as a beautiful picture book they produce every year.

After connecting with them and gifting them a copy of my book, they asked if *The Unexpected Journey* would be part of the packages they give to the expecting families. With this collaboration, my book is something the parents have for themselves and the feedback has been incredible. They really have enjoyed our journey and have told us it's been great to have something for them to read and see how another family has enjoyed their new life in the world of disability. From time to time, I get a phone call that they need a new batch of books sent out to them for their care packages which means regular and recurring books sales for me.

I am now working together with many other groups and families, I am writing articles for many different platforms and also working on my second book which I feel will also be a great resource to many.

We all go through many unexpected journeys and I really look forward to what the future holds with this new journey I am on, especially with the ongoing support from Natasa and the Ultimate 48 Hour Author Team.

Nicole Guevara – Author of *Breakaway*

Discount business cards to your interviewees
(Strategy before the book was even released.)

My book, *Breakaway: An International Medical Graduate's Guide to Powerful Career Alternatives from Medicine* consists of several interviews of medical doctors who pivoted to an alternative career. If your book involves interviews, this marketing strategy is for you.

To thank the interviewees for their participation and for sharing their personal stories and experiences, the interviewee will receive a copy of the book for free and 20 to 50 discount business cards. Your interviewees will be ambassadors for your book. Without a doubt, the interviewee will share with their network that they were featured in the book. They will tell their friends, families and colleagues about their participation.

They will encourage their network to read and share their story. Their networks are your potential buyers. In order to capitalise from this word of mouth marketing, it is thoughtful to create and give discount business cards to have a tangible promotional piece for the book.

The discount business card will consist of the following information: cover of the book, discount code, website and social media platform handles. This business card will be small enough to be carried in a wallet. It can be readily available to supplement that conversation between the interviewee and the potential buyer.

It will be a visual reminder to their network to check out their story and their chapter. With the discount, it will give an additional incentive to buy the book directly from you, the author, versus from actual or online bookstores (who take a portion of your sale). In turn, there is a higher chance of having a higher return from investment.

Leah Smith – Author of *Profitable Practitioner*

Social media superstar

Social media is crucial! I'm a firm believer in social proof so I used my Facebook profile and my Facebook business pages to cross promote during my pre-launch to my official launch.

I believe that video marketing is the secret as it creates the know, like and trust factor because your potential clients can see you, hear your voice and decide if you are someone they should 'Know, Like and Trust'. I did videos on the book overview and progress throughout my pre-launch phase.

At pre-launch I also did a giveaway for my online course that I'd created that extends on the teachings of my book and this was a random draw for anyone who had purchased my book during pre-launch at retreat.

Once launched, I put the testimonials in my book into Facebook posts to share across my platforms to create this social proof that I was someone worth listening too. I also did videos when my book proof copy arrived and when my bulk order arrived.

Once I had my bulk print book, we had a book launch with three authors in my area and cross promoted our books through all of our Facebook profiles and also engaged local media coverage through Channel 7, ABC radio and *The Daily Mercury* newspaper.

Next, I contacted companies that the book would be relevant to and offered bulk orders at a discounted rate. I have also scheduled some webinars for different companies which upsell my book and course. Further, I contacted my local university and offered to give a copy of my book to each student in the graduating year of my profession and a university prize of my course for the student who meets the criteria that most related to my book topic.

Jennifer Emmett – Author of *Beyond Possible*

Invite your village to share your authoring journey
Through my Ultimate 48 Hour Author journey, I started to understand the power of social media in relation to creating book sales and building my new business. I had previously been an extremely haphazard Facebook user and my profile did not portray the image I wanted.

I completely revamped my personal profile page. I moved my family and close friend discussions into private Facebook groups and opened up my personal profile page to the world.

I spent an afternoon taking photos of myself on my mobile phone, using a cheap phone stand and a plain coloured wall as the backdrop. My android phone has a 'Show Palm' shooting mode. That means I just need to show the camera my palm and it will count down a couple of sections and then take the shot. I took photos of myself in lots of different stances and facial expressions. I then used these photos over a number of weeks for the pre-release teaser posts and progress updates. It worked a treat, I sold over 70 books before it was released and my little Facebook Village (about 160 friends at the time) started to grow. If you already have a large following you could generate hundreds of pre-release sales.

I also invited people to help me with the editing of the book. Ten people quickly jumped onboard and videoed themselves reading a chapter and posted the video in a closed Facebook group name Beyond Possible – Jennifer Emmett. Unbeknownst to me at the time, this turned out to be a stroke of brilliance. Out of those ten people, seven of them chose to participate in beta testing **The Good Life Game Plan**, which is the program I wrote as companion to the book. These seven people then told their friends about the program and my business is starting to grow.

I have shared some images of my Facebook posts and Good Life Game Plan crew on my Beyond Possible landing page and encourage you to share your authoring journey with your village.

Renae Kunda – Co-Author of *King of the Cape*

Make friends and influence sales!
I've been running a motorcycle tour in Cape York for 30 years and we've built up a pretty good social following in that time, but I didn't really know how to use it until I met Natasa and the Ultimate 48 Hour Author team. You see I was always very, very professional and used our social media as a business brochure. Then I heard the words, 'Be "SOCIAL" on social media!' Wait, what – WOW!

1. **Plan your posts before typing them**

   DING, DING, DING this is my biggest problem, I have news now and like any good gossip girl I want to share it right now and see what everyone else thinks of the idea ... Stop! THINK! I try to always schedule my posts in advance now to help curb me away from impatience and wasted posts.

2. **Create questions**

   Sometimes a perfectly planned and executed story over a couple of days or posts is way more fun for your 'social friends and colleagues'. Think of ways to tease your readers a little bit and keep them wondering and asking questions.

3. **PICK the PICTURE!**

   Pictures tell a thousand words so make them great, don't use the grainy ghost because someone moved, that just says all the wrong things. If you just missed the shot, you missed it! Don't use it.

4. **Find a bigger audience**

   Lastly, think about who this post is going to relate to and find big sites that focus on that audience and tag them. I like to send a message to these big sites and ask if I can tag them.

   This last little tip helped me to build a rapport with the people running the social media for those big sites that matter to my business and I know their first names now.

   The big tip is – be social on social media and use the message button, people like to chat.

Kim Stevenson – Author of *Dare to Dream*

I made 21K in 24 hours, sitting in my living room doing what I love

One of the areas that Natasa talks about is working with people who align with your values. I reached out to ASN because they run an online women's chat group supporting women through their health and nutrition goals. Being part of that group, I saw numerous posts in the group by women challenged by emotional eating.

Being my niche, I had to help. This is my calling. My love. My passion. I reached out to the manager of the group and offered to do a one-hour Facebook live answering any questions about emotional eating. I provided them with my speaker bio which was already created from Natasa's in-house designer following the strategy she has shared earlier in the book.

There was a two-week lead in time which allowed for participants to submit their questions earlier. This gave me the foundation for the first part of the Facebook live. I could prewrite responses to ensure that I could deliver extreme value and align content to my book. ASN took care of the marketing and posts engagement both on Facebook and Instagram. I simply commented occasionally.

On the night I went through all the pre-empted questions and then opened up the floor to further questions so that I could help and interact with people live. I used as many opportunities as possible to reference activities in my book. By planting the seed, participants had a taste for what was in my book, how it could help them, giving emotional buy in as to why they needed to purchase the book.

To increase post engagement after the Facebook live, I offered five copies of my book to be given away. To be eligible to go in the draw, participants were asked to post their takeaways and breakthroughs from the Facebook live. This increased engagement in the group and interest in my book. I had numerous enquiries about how to purchase the book as well. Both the manager of the group and myself were posting the link to my book. Having the manager of the group give her endorsement also raised the credibility encouraging people to purchase it.

I sold 23 copies in 24 hours following the Facebook live and got four new clients which was $21,000 in total sales!

Dr Jo Lukins – Author of *The Elite* and *In the Grandstands*

The paperback lamington drive

Selling your book into the networks of others is an easy strategy that broadens the reach of your market. I have successfully achieved this through a win-win promotion for selling through affiliates (association/club/school/charity).

Affiliate marketing is a performance-based selling method where an affiliate earns money or service by promoting and selling your book and other products. The advantage for the affiliate is that they can raise funds without holding any stock, having to fulfil orders or deal with customer services.

For my recent book, *In the Grandstands* I offer it as a product for sporting associations to promote to their members.

1) Research potential affiliates (think beyond your immediate location)
2) Reach terms on:
    a) Type of commission (will it be monetary or will you provide a service, e.g. deliver a seminar?)
    b) If monetary, determine a fixed fee per sale or % commission on sales
    c) Time frame – will the promotion be for a set period or ongoing?
    d) Agree on the distribution (will you post copies or deliver in bulk to the affiliate for them to distribute?)
3) Set up the affiliate with a unique landing page. Be clear on the page that part funds of sale will be channelled back to the association
4) The affiliate promotes the landing page (through a newsletter, social media, etc.)
5) You track and deliver according to agreement
6) You pay the commission according to the agreement.

Krissy Regan – Author of *Broken to Unbreakable*

Roadshow fun

A strategy that I have successfully implemented is to seek out events, retail shops, websites, business groups, networking groups, online groups, etc. where my target audience would be. My book sits across a few different categories including Health, Wellbeing, Self-help, Personal Development and Spiritual Development.

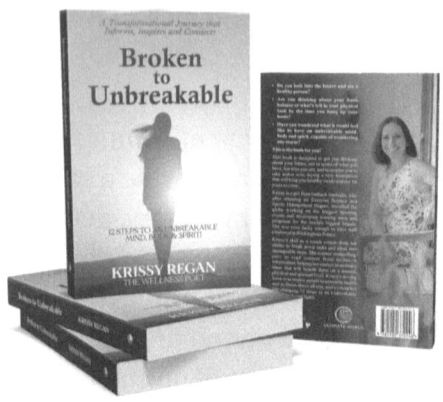

I looked broadly at online, offline, print and digital media and managed to create a wide following for my work domestically and internationally.

In 2020 we had to think outside the box, and as a result new opportunities have presented themselves. I have written articles for online and printed magazines, participated in international podcasts and literature festivals, showcased my book at book fairs and approached a wide variety of different retail outlets (not just bookshops) to sell my books.

To date I have more than 20 independent retail outlets selling my book and it is available on all international commercial platforms.

One of the most successful strategies I have implemented is a Roadshow. For example, I have travelled around my regional area of North Queensland visiting other towns and cities doing a variety of activities over a 2–7 day period including: donating my book to local libraries, local media including newspapers and radio interviews, book signings in book shops, market stalls and wellness expos and hosting my own workshops.

This strategy has enabled me to reach more people in a local area, create a following and gain credibility quickly for my work. Even if I only meet a small number of people or sell a few copies of the book, I have original content from my travels that I can share and then my followers share as well, which is very helpful for book promotion. When people meet me in person, they comment how much exposure I'm getting and that they enjoy seeing where I will turn up next.

Glenda Wise – Author of *The World is Your Pearl*

FOCUS on SUCCESS by creating a LOOK
My way of conquering anything is to get ahead of the eight ball. I am an artist, an adventure traveller, and a writer; but definitely 'not' a public speaker. However, I figured that, if I, and my book were to become successful, I needed to promote myself as an entertaining speaker with plenty to offer, then 'visualise' myself as such. I needed to sneak up on it from behind and MAKE IT HAPPEN. By creating a mindset from the start, and making a decision to commit to being in it for the long haul, I made 'being a successful speaker' my focus, and it worked!!!

No matter how good my book was, it would be invisible if it sat in a box in my house, or out there in cyberspace where no-one knew where to find it. So I got three things done early before my books were even printed.

Firstly, I employed a web builder to create a catchy little website www.glendawisebooks.com, with a splash-page which directed people to buy my book from the start. With a BUY NOW button, an instant sale was possible for those interested enough to be looking while the impulse was there and the moment for a sale was not lost.

With this website in place, I sold 50 books before they were even printed, by directing people to a special pre-print promotion through social media.

Secondly, as soon as my book cover design had been created by Nik, (Ultimate 48 Hour Author's amazing designer), I decided to 'go for it' by having him design a Speaker Bio along the same lines. I wrote the blurb, and he created this flyer using the same colours, images and text as the book.

I had them printed in two sizes.

A5 size which perfect to write a personal note of thanks on the back and to be inserted inside the front of the book for the purchaser to hand on or leave lying around for someone else to pick up; and ...

A4 size which would go through my printer. These would be used in two ways, either as a poster to leave at libraries, or to include when posting the book to anyone who may prospectively know of a group who could be interested in having me at a speaking event. On the back of these, with space left at the top for me to hand write the buyers name, Dear...... I printed:

Thank you for buying my book. I hope you enjoy the read. If you know of a group interested in a speaker, please pass this on.

With my best regards,
Glenda Wise

REAL-LIFE AUTHORS GETTING REAL-LIFE RESULTS

GLENDA WISE
THE WORLD IS YOUR PEARL

'There is a way that Glenda embraces the world that is both refreshing and addictive'
~ Mary Moody ~

is an artist, illustrator and author, with a big passion for adventure. She has written and published her new book, The World is your Pearl, where she shares a few of her extreme adventures.

Outside the scope of high-end travel staying in luxury hotels and resorts, the true essence of a remote experience for Glenda requires sleeping in tents, tea houses, trucks, boats, yurts, riads, caves or tribal homes, and once under the wing of her brother's aeroplane. She has had many epic experiences through safe travel on a comparative shoestring with the right support.

After divorce from the man who remains one of her best friends, her two children having grown and left home, and the loss of her only brother in a tragic workplace accident, Glenda embarks on a completely new journey. She shares an inspiring account of how she got out into the world of adventure after loss and sadness.

Inspired by earlier experiences with her brother in the wilds of Bougainville, Glenda shifted her mind-set and now travels off the beaten track and often way out of her comfort zone. She describes some of her many amazing trips, trekking, cycling and exploring (often at altitude), visiting cultures which are remote and ancient in their customs and lifestyles.

In her exciting and engaging talks, Glenda describes:
. How to sneak up on adventure
. How to go about achieving it
. How to get started the very first time
. How to conquer your fears
. How to keep having adventures at any age
. What you'll tell your grandchildren

To enquire about engaging Glenda as a speaker at your next event, contact her below for availabilities and pricing. Glenda can adapt her talks to suit your event's timing and audience,

WWW.GLENDAWISEBOOKS.COM

PEARLYTRAVELLER@GMAIL.COM

These were hand addressed it to each individual and signed separately with my personal signature.

This was my way of beginning my speaking journey. The rest just fell into place once the commitment was made. I had no idea who might take up this offer, but I put it out there for any possible group who might want a speaker. I could never underestimate the power of one person's thinking. It might be the old man down the road with the idea of putting the idea to his retirement village or the lady in the shop looking for an idea for her Rotary group!

My fee, as a non-celebrity, would be for me to sell my books at the event.

(I am told however, that professional speakers of celebrity status can command *obscene* amounts of money, including air fares, transfers and four-star hotel accommodation).

I sent my flyer off to every library within driving distance from my home, with the view to arranging a time for me to be included into their quarterly program to be advertised as a speaker at their author events.

I also visited book shops to offer my books for sale and to leave a physical flyer to facilitate the setting up of future book signing events.

Thirdly, I had a bookmark designed. This served two purposes. The main one being as a business card to hand out spontaneously while talking to people and mentioning that I had just written a book; and the other, to insert into each book as an added gift to buyers so that they could either keep it or possibly pass it on to others.

On the back of the bookmark I included my website. You have to spend money to make money, and this 'packaging' from the 'look of the book' made for professional marketing and presented me as credible from the start.

AFTERWORD

SHUT UP AND SELL YOUR FIRST BOOK

ABOUT THE AUTHOR

Natasa Denman was born and raised in Skopje, Macedonia up to the age of 14, after which she emigrated to Melbourne, Australia to be with her mum. They were separated for two and a half years. She didn't speak English and found it challenging in the first two years to fit into the new country and culture. Her zest for learning and achievement fast-tracked this process and she had high performance results in her academic endeavours.

Natasa has a Bachelor of Applied Science (Psychology/Psychophysiology), Diploma in Life Coaching, NLP Practitioner Certification, Practitioner of Matrix Therapies, holds a Black Belt in Taekwondo and is a Professional Certified Coach (PCC) through the International Coaching Federation.

Being creative and writing books is something she never planned to do. Her passion for business and marketing was the reason she wrote her first book *The 7 Ultimate Secrets to Weight Loss* in June 2011. This book put her first business on the map and enabled her husband to join her full-time in the business a year later. She has also written *Ultimate 48 Hour Author*, *Ultimate 48 Hour Author (fully revised edition)*, *Shut Up and Write Your First Book*, *Natasa Denman Reveals... 1000 Days to a Million Dollar Coaching Business from Home*, *Fully Booked Retreats*, is a contributor of *You Can... Live the Life of Your Dreams* and *Speaking Successfully*, and is a co-author of *Ninja Couch Marketing*, *Bums on Seats*, *Me and my VA* and *Guilt Free Parents*.

Ultimate 48 Hour Author came about as a result of the success books have brought to Natasa's business. Aside from books, she has also written five programs and has three licensed systems that are being utilised by others internationally in their businesses.

She is now known as The Ultimate 48 Hour Author. Natasa is a highly sought-after professional speaker (CSP accredited) and

ABOUT THE AUTHOR

Australia's leading authority on helping first-time authors publish their books. She has helped over 550 solopreneurs become first-time published authors in the last seven years in Australia, USA, Canada, New Zealand and UAE. She also has clients from 10 other international countries.

In 11 years of business, Natasa has been nominated for The Telstra Businesswoman of the Year twice and was a finalist in AusMumpreneur of the Year in Product Innovation.

Appearing in all major media outlets across Australia including the *Sydney Morning Herald*, the *Financial Review* and *The Age*, Natasa is changing the way people do business in Australia and the world. She now runs a multiple seven-figure business with her husband and three children, travelling the world, spreading her message and helping small businesses thrive. Natasa's mum has now also joined the business.

In 2018, Natasa expanded the business and opened up her own in-house publishing company *Ultimate World Publishing*. This was a huge move for everyone as the business further grew to include the ability to offer publishing packages to clients. Natasa's clients are now writing their second and third books with the company, and beyond.

In 2020, the fully offline touring and event business that Ultimate 48 Hour Author was, fully pivoted to an online model due to the coronavirus pandemic. The team and family have never looked back since. The businesses are thriving and they get to help even more people regularly on a global scale.

The Denman family's passion is to continue to build this as a fully-fledged family business helping thousands around the world become first-time authors without compromising on also living a balanced lifestyle. Their motto is Work Hard – Play Hard, whereby they work intensely for five and half months in the year, spend two and a half months on building new systems to add value to what they do, and travel and holiday for the remaining four months of the year. While there is a pause on travel they decided to set up house on the Gold Coast in Queensland and run the business from two locations, being totally location independent.

This is what they want to enable others to create when building their own entrepreneurial ventures with the help of a published book.

Ultimate 48 Hour Author lives by four values: Fun, Fast, Fame and above all FAMILY.

Natasa's websites:
    www.natasadenman.com
    www.writeabook.com.au

Email: natasa@natasadenman.com

EXPLORE

- Want to discover if you should write a book this year?
- Unsure on how to put the pieces of the puzzle together?

If you are ready to begin your author journey but are still on the fence if it is worth your time and effort, here is the best place to start.

1. Join our amazing **Author Your Way to Riches** Facebook group and be a part of a community of thousands of others that are on the same journey as you. Ask questions, learn from their experiences, and arm yourself with all the information you need to help you decide your next steps.

AUTHOR YOUR WAY TO RICHES - FACEBOOK GROUP

https://tinyurl.com/authoryourwaytoriches

2. Join our Ultimate 48 Hour Author Academy for **FREE**. Access trainings and enjoy exclusive member only access to the hottest resources we have available to help you overcome your procrastination and self-doubt.

THE ULTIMATE 48 HOUR AUTHOR ACADEMY

https://ultimate48hourauthor.teachable.com

ACCELERATE

Writing a book is important to you – and so should making an impact with it be! You don't want to be one of those people with a garage full of books. You don't want to be the best kept secret.

You want to get your book out there. To build your profile, credibility, and leverage your book to its full potential.

Here is your chance to LEVEL UP.

1. Attend our game-changing **Blueprint for Book Writing Success Seminar**. Attended by thousands of people from more than 15 countries, this live and interactive seminar teaches the exact blueprint to write, publish and leverage your first book.

REGULAR LIVE SEMINARS FOR AUSTRALIA and USA/CANADA TIME ZONES, BOOK YOUR SPOT HERE:
https://writeabook.com.au/writing-workshops/

2. The Proven Book Writing Success Formula. **Our Ultimate Book Planner** is your first-class ticket to your book's completion. With all the templates, systems, and mentoring at your fingertips, gone is the confusion and disorganisation that plagues most first-time authors. With this planner, it is time to make your book a reality!

ENTER CODE **ACCELERATE** to RECEIVE $10 OFF at CHECKOUT
https://writeabook.com.au/shop/

DOMINATE

Already done much of the hard work and ready to share your message on a global scale?

1. If you are ready to self-publish, Ultimate World Publishing is your best option. With a dedicated publications manager and world-class editors, design, and layout teams, your book will be bookstore quality and reflect your personality and brand. With Ultimate World Publishing, 'It is Your Book, Your Way'.

BOOK A CHAT WITH OUR PUBLISHING TEAM
https://writeabook.com.au/ultimate-world-publishing/

2. The pinnacle of our **Ultimate 48 Hour Author** experience is our **3-Day Virtual Retreat**. By application only, this bespoke experience is the guaranteed way to become the published author you want to be. More than 500 people can't be wrong!

It is an experience like no other and combines industry leading:

- Education
- Masterminding
- Mentoring
- Writing blocks, and of course
- A whole lot of fun along the way!

TO SEE IF THE RETREAT IS RIGHT FOR YOU –
BOOK A CHAT TODAY
https://tinyurl.com/authorqualifyingchat

NOTES

www.ingramcontent.com/pod-product-compliance
Lightning Source LLC
Chambersburg PA
CBHW021147080526
44588CB00008B/250